PIE 'N' MASH
&
PREFABS

PIE 'N' MASH
&
PREFABS

MY 1950s CHILDHOOD

NORMAN JACOBS

JOHN BLAKE

Published by John Blake Publishing Ltd,
3 Bramber Court, 2 Bramber Road,
London W14 9PB, England

www.johnblakepublishing.co.uk

www.facebook.com/johnblakebooks ⨍
twitter.com/jblakebooks ⓔ

This edition published in 2015

ISBN: 978-1-78418-123-9

British Library Cataloguing-in-Publication Data:

A catalogue record for this book is available from the British Library.

Design by www.envydesign.co.uk

Printed in Great Britain by CPI Group (UK) Ltd

1 3 5 7 9 10 8 6 4 2

Papers used by John Blake Publishing are natural, recyclable products made from
wood grown in sustainable forests. The manufacturing processes conform to the
environmental regulations of the country of origin.

Every attempt has been made to contact the relevant copyright-holders,
but some were unobtainable. We would be grateful if the appropriate
people could contact us.

CONTENTS

ACKNOWLEDGEMENTS

First and foremost, I should like to thank my parents not just for giving me a very secure and happy childhood but also because before they died both of them wrote down their own memories to pass on. I have found these to be of enormous help in triggering my own memory especially of my very early days.

I would also like to thank various people both at Graham Maw Christie and John Blake Publishing for their encouragement, support, advice and suggestions especially Jane Graham Maw, Alice Smales, Anna Marx and Jane Donovan.

CHAPTER ONE

WELFARE ORANGE AND MALT

'Mummy, my leg!'

When Mum opened the door to my seven-year-old brother, it looked as though his leg was hanging on just by the skin at the back of his knee. He'd been crossing a bomb site, not unusual then in the East End, when he fell down a hole. That morning he'd gone to school in a pair of white plimsolls, but now had one white one and one red one.

Although I was due to be born that day, my hugely pregnant mum picked him up, her only thought being to get him to hospital as fast as possible; but Hackney Hospital was about a mile away. Home phones were still a rarity. She sat him in the armchair and ran out into the street, grabbed a passer-by and asked if he could phone for an ambulance from the phone box just down the street. Five minutes later, waiting with John and

1

panicking that the man hadn't done as she asked, she dashed out into the street again just as a lorry was coming along, waving her arms frantically to stop it. The driver had to brake hard to miss her, screeching to a juddering halt. He jumped out.

'What on earth...' He was ready to give her a piece of his mind but stopped when he saw the heavily pregnant, tearful woman waving her arms about like a windmill.

'My little boy,' she sobbed, 'his leg... Can you take him to hospital?'

As soon as he saw the state John was in, he didn't hesitate: he carried him into the lorry and drove him and Mum (and me, I suppose!) straight to the hospital. Then he carried him into casualty and laid him on a bed. It was only then that John started to cry; he hadn't cried or spoken up till then. In spite of all the blood, he was found to be suffering from no more than a very deep cut to his knee, which required eleven stitches.

I suppose, with all this going on, Mum forgot about giving birth to me on the due date.

I eventually arrived four days later at 8am on Monday, 19 May 1947, weighing 9lb 3oz and with a full shock of thick black hair. John was still in the children's ward, and a nurse informed him he had a new baby brother. He wasn't impressed.

While the three of us were in hospital, Dad was back at home having to fend for himself, and not making a very good job of it. In those days, it was normal for wives to cook and clean and take on all the household burdens, so he hadn't had much practice. Luckily, our neighbours took pity on him and provided him with meals between his visits to the hospital and going to work. I don't think he did much else for the better part of a week until we all finally came home to Millfield Terrace.

Our prefab was one of just seven in a row, known as Millfield Terrace, set back a few yards from Millfields Road, the long street linking Clapton Pond and Hackney Marshes. The prefabs – short for 'prefabricated buildings' – were situated on Millfields, a 20-acre area of open parkland, which lay between Chatsworth Road and Clapton Greyhound Stadium and stretched right back to the River Lea and the boundary with Leyton. Each of the seven prefabs had its own path leading up from the road, while along the pavement a small iron railing separated the road from the field. By the time my parents arrived, the only prefab left was the one at the end, so our address became 7 Millfield Terrace.

John told me later the main thing he remembered about moving in was Mum and Dad's fear that the other residents of Millfields Road might think they were squatters, not real tenants. But they were real tenants all right, with a rent card to prove it. The rent was 16s 8d (83p) per week including rates, water and electricity charges.

At that time, just after the Second World War, thousands of couples and families had no homes of their own and had to live in rented rooms with shared facilities, or with parents and in-laws. Overcrowding and lack of privacy were real problems, so for many families prefabs offered, for the first time, a proper modern home, better than any they could have dared hope for or aspire to before. The 1944 Temporary Housing Act had brought them in as a quick solution to the housing crisis caused by both bomb damage and a general need to clear away the nineteenth-century slums of the East End. All the parts of these temporary houses were pre-built in a factory and then put together in kit style on site, making them quick and easy to erect.

There were a number of different styles; ours was the Arcon Mark V. Designed by the Ministry of Works, it was built as a tubular steel frame with corrugated asbestos cement cladding and a curved roof apex. The dangers of asbestos were unknown at that time and it was felt to be a useful building material as it was fire resistant and provided good insulation.

Inside, the prefab was built round a central core consisting of a large kitchen, bathroom and separate WC. There was a large living room and two bedrooms. The fitted kitchen came with a built-in fridge (something that most families still did not possess), a cooker, a sink with running hot and cold water, a roomy larder and a pull-down table. We never used the pull-down table as we had our own table, which we placed in front of the window, and we ate all meals as a family around it. There was also the copper, a wash boiler with wringer attached, where Mum boiled up her whites with the aid of some Reckitt's Blue, a product widely used in pre-washing-machine days as a whitener.

The front door opened into a small passageway, which led directly to the toilet, the bathroom and the two bedrooms, but we preferred to use the side door leading straight into the kitchen and living room, which we called the 'big room'. And it was a big room too. As well as our three-piece suite centred round the open fire, a console television and a large wooden table, we also managed to fit in a six-foot-long mahogany sideboard and a secretaire consisting of a drop-down desk and three bookcases. Both were made to order and intricately carved by my father. We also had a radiogram, a substantial piece of wooden furniture in its own right. Made by EKCO, a Southend wireless and television manufacturing firm, it measured about three feet in height and two feet six inches in width. There was a lid on top, which opened to reveal a turntable on one side and a wireless tuner on the other. The rest of the space was taken up with the speakers.

Outside was a large garden, both front and back, with a brick shed in the back garden housing a galvanised coal bin.

My family were the ideal candidates for one of these new homes. When my father went into the army shortly after the outbreak of war in 1939, my mother and brother left the East End of London to escape the bombing and stayed with relatives in Middlesex and Hertfordshire. Dad was called up at the start of the War and served in the Royal Artillery as a bombardier in charge of a small anti-aircraft unit. He saw very little action and spent most of the War in places like Taunton and Clacton-on-Sea practising firing his big Bofors gun into the sky at imaginary German Dornier and Heinkel bombers. After D-Day came in 1944, he was sent to the Netherlands to help Dutch families readjust to normal life after the occupation.

Although not once throughout the War did he manage to shoot down any enemy planes – I can't, in all honesty, claim that my dad 'won the War' – I am sure the part he played was just as valuable as anyone else's. When it finished, they settled back in the East End, living with my father's parents and several grown-up children in a small, cramped flat in Cookham Buildings in Shoreditch. In 1946, the London County Council

(L.C.C.) allocated them one of the new prefabs in Hackney and they eagerly grabbed the opportunity.

At first, Dad worked as a woodcarver for a furniture company, but very soon he set up in business on his own in Columbia Road, Bethnal Green. His main stock-in-trade was carving tables and chair legs, creating his own designs, and in the late forties and fifties, he picked up a lot of work from local cabinet makers. Bethnal Green and Shoreditch were then the centre of the wood trade and there were many small, independent businesses providing the large shops with furniture. People needed new furniture after the War, because they had either moved house or been bombed out; this meant that the woodcarving trade was a good business to be in, and we lived in reasonable comfort for a working-class family.

Although the design part of Dad's job was very artistic, the actual carving was hard manual labour, which built up his arm muscles so he was very strong. He was a handsome man with thick black hair, standing just under six feet tall; Mum often remarked that he bore a strong resemblance to the film star Robert Taylor. At five feet seven, Mum was fairly tall. She was very good-looking, blonde with blue eyes, although part of her right eye was brown. During the war years, she had learnt to be very independent, having to cope with John on her own while Dad was away in the army. Although Dad took command in most situations and gave the orders, she didn't really take too much notice of him and carried on in her own way, letting him think he was in control, but really it was Mum who was in charge.

My earliest memory is of Dad bathing me in the kitchen sink. Although I felt very safe and secure in his arms, I did think it was a bit strange to be in the sink because that's where Mum washed the dishes and I normally went in the bath. Mum must have gone out and left him to do it. Goodness knows why he chose the kitchen sink, but I must have been very young to fit in there. Another vivid early memory is of sitting on Dad's lap in front of the fire when my uncle Bill came to visit. As they talked, one of my white socks became loose and started to hang off my foot and I stroked it up and down against the fireplace, watching it get blacker and blacker from the soot.

I was always put to bed for a midday nap, and when I woke up it would be time for *Listen With Mother* on the wireless.

'The time is a quarter to two. This is the BBC Home Service for mothers and children at home. Are you ready for the music? When it stops, Catherine Edwards will be here to speak to you. Ding-de-dong. Ding-de-dong, Ding, ding! Are you sitting comfortably? Then I'll begin!'

So began a fifteen-minute programme of stories, songs and nursery rhymes for children under five. I used to love every minute of it, listening quietly with Mum. Another of the storytellers was Daphne Oxenford; what a lovely-sounding name it was to my young ears.

We bought our first television on 19 September 1949. Not many people had television in those days; many parts of the country were unable to receive signals as there were only two transmitters, one at Alexandra Palace for the London area and another at Sutton Coldfield for the Midlands. The television we had was a 10" Murphy console costing £71 10s 8d. As I was only two, I can't remember a time when we didn't have a television.

Watch with Mother started in 1950 when I was three. There was Andy Pandy, a puppet who lived in a basket with his friends, Teddy and Looby Loo, and later on, Bill and Ben, the Flowerpot Men. Another favourite of mine from that period was Prudence Kitten, little cat puppets in dresses, presented by Annette Mills.

The television was bought from a shop called J. H. Dunkley and Son Ltd in Lower Clapton Road. Those still being somewhat pioneering days of television, the set frequently went wrong and we'd have to call the shop to send someone round to repair it. The engineer normally chosen for this task was a man called Lassman. He would remove the back, look inside, tap this, tighten that, trace one wire here, another there but usually all to no avail. The workings of the television and why it had gone wrong seemed as big a mystery to him as it did to us. After a few more plucky attempts to get it going – he was nothing if not persistent – he would confess to being a wireless man and say that he didn't know much about televisions. Inevitably, the set would have to go back to the shop to be repaired there. Whenever a TV engineer was called on and Lassman arrived, we knew we'd be without a television for at least a couple of days.

The other major regular event in our lives occurred every Thursday and Saturday evening: dog racing nights at Clapton Greyhound Stadium.

Clapton Stadium was built in 1900 to house Clapton Orient Football Club. When the new craze for greyhound racing arrived in this country in the late 1920s, the Millfields Road ground was converted to a greyhound stadium at a cost of over

£80,000, a big sum of money in those days. It held its first race night on 7 April 1928 and, because of the amount of money now invested in greyhounds, the football team was soon asked to find a new home and moved away, eventually becoming Leyton Orient.

Our prefab was right next door to Clapton Stadium so we certainly knew all about it on Thursday and Saturday evenings.

'The dark-and-late motors are coming,' I used to say to my brother, peering outside.

'They're taxis, stupid,' was his normal reply.

Hundreds of them deposited their customers near the bottom of our path, while hundreds more people converged on the stadium on foot. Millfields Road and all the other roads nearby would be lined with cars belonging to the more affluent dog racing supporters.

Once a race was underway, we could hear the roar of the crowd from inside our house, rising in crescendo as the race neared its conclusion. Then there'd be silence for half an hour or so until the next race. I wanted nothing more than to be there myself, and imagined the huge stadium with the men in their flat caps and the spotlights as a kind of heaven for grown-ups.

Every race night, I would be sent off by Dad to the disabled vendor seated in an invalid carriage outside the stadium entrance to buy two packets of Larkins peanuts. Breaking open the shells and eating these delicacies was one of the highlights of Dad's week. Living right next door to the stadium had its advantages.

On special occasions, we were allowed into the stadium. The big race of the year was the Scurry Cup, one that in its heyday rivalled even the Derby in terms of prestige. Staged over 400 yards, it attracted the fastest greyhounds in the land, and the list of winners through the years reads like a who's who of sprinting. Scurry Cup evening always finished with a big fireworks display to which everyone was admitted free of charge and, naturally, we would be first in the queue. One year, they let us in before the last race. I must have been about nine or ten and I picked a greyhound to win because it had a nice red coat. It duly won, but John wasn't impressed as I danced around, sticking my tongue out at him and chanting, 'I'm the winner! I'm the winner!'

As I was growing up, I got to know all our neighbours in the other six prefabs. We residents mostly got on very well together as there was a real sense of community between us, something that I think is largely lost between neighbours today. Dad was a great one for giving people nicknames and I think it was many years before I knew all their actual names – in fact, I don't think I ever knew the real names of some of them. In our row of prefabs, starting at number one we had the not very imaginative 'Number One', whose real names were George and Phyllis Yewman. George worked for the *Daily Mirror*. 'Number One' applied to both of them, so you had to work out which one was being talked about by the context. George and Phyllis were both very untidy and things were strewn about all over their house. They had two children, Petula and Mark, both born after me.

Number Two housed Charlie and Ann Tickton with their daughter Pat and sons Alan, Barry and baby Keith. Ann's nickname was 'Polly' because, whenever Mum popped in to see her, Ann would always say, 'I'll put the kettle on.' Keith was known as 'Ki-Ki' and he came in useful whenever there was a thunderstorm. 'Don't worry, Norman,' Mum would reassure me. 'It's only Ki-Ki's mother having coal delivered.'

The Willets, Tom and Mary, lived at number three with their twins, Colin and Barbara. Colin had flaming red hair while Barbara's was jet black. Mary's nickname, probably not hard to guess, was 'Twinny'.

At number four were Vic and his wife, Molly. They had three children, Sylvia, Pat and Terrence. Vic was a bit thin on top, earning himself the nickname 'Baldy', which at some point evolved into 'Bally', which is how I always knew him. One of the first things Bally did on moving into the prefab was to remove the pilot light from the immersion heater to save money.

Tom and Joan lived at number five with their son, Richard. Tom was a motorcycle policeman and, although he changed jobs within a year of moving in to become a P.E. teacher at Hackney Downs Grammar School, forever after he was known as 'Copper'. Richard would be called in from playing outside on most Sundays to have his 'marmalade tea'.

Next door to us at number six lived the one and only 'Bandy Bertha' Rogers, whose great hobby seemed to consist of distributing bowls of chicken soup, unsolicited, up and down the row of prefabs. A veritable walking soup kitchen, she was, to put it mildly, a character. Any neighbourhood without such a woman was definitely missing out. At a time when the Government was nationalising all its major services and utilities for the benefit of the country, we felt that she too should have been nationalised and made available to all the citizens of this fine land but fate had decreed we should have her all to ourselves. An East End Jewess, she was small and plump, and in no way suited her real name, Sybil. She was definitely a born Bertha. Her husband, Geoffrey, and her son, David, were in their own way characters as well but nothing to compare with the magnitude of the woman of the house.

Bertha and Geoffrey were both ex-RAF and before coming to the prefabs had been squatting in a disused Air Force hut. Having got married during the War, when peace came, Geoffrey seemed bemused by the situation he now found himself in and must have wondered what on earth had possessed him to marry such a woman. His mother lived in Sawbridgeworth, Hertfordshire, and, when visiting her son, deplored the disaster he had brought upon himself. Bertha was most definitely not her idea of a daughter-in-law. Sawbridgeworth was probably quite unaware that such people existed. Bertha's dedication to her chicken soup knew no bounds. One day, she came round to ask us if she could borrow some vermicelli for the soup. 'But only if it is Rakusen's,' she insisted. 'Otherwise I won't have it.'

If you stood at our front door and looked out, there was a neat terraced row of Victorian houses over the other side of Millfields Road, between two side roads called Chippendale Street and Sewdley Street. If you stood at their front doors, you would have seen our little prefabs blocking their once-clear view of the green Millfields. I don't know what they thought of our group of seven more or less homeless families moving into these new-fangled prefabs. Maybe they should have received a rate rebate, except, of course, for those living opposite Bertha, who should have had an extra entertainment tax levied on them.

Perhaps the only owner who didn't mind the arrival of the new families was Peter Curtis, who owned the off-licence that stood directly opposite us on the corner of Chippendale Street and Millfields Road. My parents didn't drink but we would use the 'offy' to buy a bottle of something every Sunday to go with lunch, usually Tizer, R. White's Cola or Cream Soda or Succulent Lemonade. We also used to buy vinegar there, which was stored in a large barrel on the counter. We'd have to take our own empty bottle, which would be filled by vinegar drawn off from the cask. I don't remember us ever buying pre-bottled vinegar as you would these days.

Next door to the off-licence lived 'Ginger', 'Monkey' and their daughter, Christine. Ginger I think is obvious as she had bright-red hair. Monkey was a small hunchback, and his was the only nickname Dad came up with that he later admitted was very unkind. In the early days, Ginger was often to be seen with an enamel jug in her hand, going up to the café round the corner in Chatsworth Road to get some readymade tea as packets of tea were still on ration.

The woman living next to Ginger was the only person in this stretch of the road on either side, apart from Peter Curtis, not to have a nickname. In fact, she didn't have a name at all that I ever knew but that was because no one ever talked about her. She was a single woman living on her own who seemed to have a long succession of men calling at her door, morning, noon and night. I didn't see her very often as she spent most of her time indoors but occasionally she would stand in her front yard, smoking a cigarette. It was difficult to tell how old she was but she always wore an off-the-shoulder tight and low-cut sweater as well as an even tighter black knee-length skirt. What really struck me was her extremely light blonde hair and her bright-red lipstick; being very young I had no idea why the neighbours never mentioned her in polite conversation...

The next family along was the Lanes: Leslie, Rhoda, Leslie Junior and Colin. Collectively, they were known as 'the Laneys', but Rhoda had her own nickname of 'Ee-lo' because that would be her standard greeting, morning, noon and night.

Next up was 'Gatewaller', who used to spend most of his day standing by his gate and watching the world go by. He's one whose first name I never did know. Nor did I ever find out the family's surname as his wife and two children were simply known to us as 'Gatewaller two', 'Gatewaller three' and 'Gatewaller four'. One day, we saw a wedding car outside their house and, not long after, 'Gatewaller five', husband of Gatewaller three, moved in to be followed in rapid succession by baby Gatewallers, numbers six, seven, eight, nine and ten.

Next door to this ever-expanding family lived 'Old Daddy Flat Cap' and his brood, which consisted of his wife and two children. He was never seen out in public without his flat cap on, hence the name. One day, in the mid-1950s, a red car appeared outside his door and this became Old Daddy Flat Cap's pride and joy. He would spend hours washing it, polishing it, cleaning out the inside and generally lavishing great care and attention on it. He did everything you could do with a car... except drive it. It never actually went anywhere; it just stayed on the road outside his house.

After spending untold hours on his beloved motor, he decided he had earned a holiday, so, one morning, with his flat cap still nestling firmly on his head, he set off by foot, with a brown paper parcel tucked securely under his arm, to recuperate from his efforts and renew his strength so that he could once again return to work on his red car and make it a credit to his flat cap. His wife and children waved him off from the front door as he wended his way up Millfields Road and continued to wave until he was lost from sight. About a fortnight later, Old Daddy Flat Cap returned with the brown paper parcel still securely tucked under his arm, fit and raring to get started on his car again. From that day to the day when we finally left our prefab, about ten years later, he continued to wash and polish his car. It stood outside, never leaving the kerbside, gleaming in the sunlight as a fine tribute to Old Daddy Flat Cap and his dedicated hours of work.

Although he never went anywhere in it, Old Daddy Flat Cap's car was the only one parked in this stretch of road. Before the arrival of his magnificent red vehicle, not a single family owned a car in our part of the street apart from Peter, who kept a van in a lock-up garage behind his off-licence. During that period, everyone relied on public transport, even though we weren't very well served by it in our area. Car-owning families were very much in the minority, certainly among the working-class families in that part of London.

About the time I was born, the woman who lived next door to Old Daddy Flat Cap also had a baby. One day, she and Mum got talking and she said she was bringing up her child on dried milk. As a result of this, she had a lot of empty tins at home and asked Mum if she would like any as they made useful containers.

After this conversation, her nickname fate was sealed and she became 'Tin Tart'.

The last house in the row opposite our prefabs was occupied by 'Crafty' and her husband and two sons. She got her nickname because Dad thought she had very shifty-looking eyes.

Dad's penchant for nicknames came from his great love of literature and literary devices. He was an avid reader, and many's the time that, out of nowhere, he would suddenly burst into poetry and recite verses from classics by Scott or Lord Macaulay.

His favourite was *Vitai Lampada* by Sir Henry Newbolt, which he used to recite in full whenever the fancy took him. He said he could always remember this poem because it was printed on a poster that used to hang in his school (Virginia Road School, Bethnal Green). I think it also appealed to his love of cricket as it began:

> There's a breathless hush in the Close to-night –
> Ten to make and the match to win –
> A bumping pitch and a blinding light,
> An hour to play and the last man in.

Each verse finished with the line, 'Play up! play up! and play the game!', which I think he took as his philosophy on life. I heard this poem so many times that I could also recite it in full by the time I went to school.

This love of poetry and literature stood Dad in good stead as he won a couple of competitions using his literary skill. The first was when a company called Berkeley asked for an advertising slogan for their new brand of luxury armchairs. His entry was:

> *Berkeley Chairs beside the fire*
> *Make mum madam, make dad sire.*

Dad won the second prize of £5.

He also won a second prize of £5 when a new chocolate biscuit called Bandit was launched. Once again, the competition was to find an advertising slogan and Dad came up with '*Bandit – Once tried always wanted*'.

The first major single event I can remember is the Festival of Britain. This took place over the summer of 1951, just after my fourth birthday, exactly one hundred years after the Great Exhibition of 1851, the intention of which had been to show that Great Britain was the world's leading industrial country. The motive behind the 1951 Festival, however, was somewhat different.

In the late 1940s and early 1950s, much of London was still in ruins as a result of the Second World War and redevelopment was badly needed. The Festival was intended to give Britons a sense of recovery and progress and to promote better-quality design in the rebuilding of British towns and cities. The Festival of Britain described itself as 'one united act of national reassessment, and one corporate reaffirmation of faith in the nation's future'. Gerald Barry, the festival director, described it as 'a tonic to the nation'. It gave a major boost to the nation's morale at a time when austerity-hit Britain most needed it.

The Festival took place all over the country, but the main

centrepiece was the South Bank Exhibition near Waterloo in London, which demonstrated Britain's advances in science, technology and industrial design. The Exhibition featured the Royal Festival Hall and the iconic Skylon, an unusual cigar-shaped aluminium-clad steel tower supported by cables, which became the abiding symbol of the Festival. Its base was nearly 15 metres (49 feet) from the ground, with the top nearly 90 metres (295 feet) high.

We travelled to the South Bank by tram, catching the 33 from Shoreditch. This was not the first time I had travelled by tram nor was it to be the last as trams were at that time a common means of travel around London. I used to like them because they seemed to me to be very exciting, rattling along the rails on their own dedicated tracks, overtaking all the other traffic and then diving down into the Kingsway Tunnel. It was all so thrilling. But best of all was when the tram reached the end of its journey, the conductor would go along pushing the wooden slatted seatbacks back across the seat so that the tram was ready to travel in the opposite direction without having to turn round. For some reason I used to find this operation absolutely fascinating.

Although the centrepiece of the Festival of Britain was on the South Bank, the part I remember fondly was the Festival Pleasure Gardens set up in Battersea Park, a few miles away. They included a restaurant with a terrace overlooking the river, Foaming Fountains, a miniature railway, the Tree-Walk consisting of a series of raised wooden walkways suspended among the tree branches and the famous 'Guinness Festival Clock'. Best of all, though, was the amusement park, which would eventually outlast all the other entertainments to become Battersea Fun Fair, only closing in the mid-1970s.

One of the major events that took place at this time was the D'Oyly Carte Gilbert & Sullivan Festival of Britain season at the Savoy Theatre, the company's original home back in the nineteenth century. Dad was a great G&S devotee and we had lots of 78 r.p.m. records at home, plus some of the brand-new 33 1/3 r.p.m. long-playing records, giving about 20–30 minutes of playing time per side, which had only been introduced in 1948. As well as playing the records, mainly on Sundays, he would sing the songs around the house and I was brought up in this tradition. When the D'Oyly Carte came to London for the Festival of Britain season, Dad took the family to see a number of the operas, *H.M.S. Pinafore*, *The Pirates of Penzance* and *Patience*. The first one we saw was *Patience* and this turned out to be quite a memorable occasion. It was the first time I had ever been to a theatre so I didn't really know what to expect. The lights dimmed and the orchestra began to play the overture. A short way into this, I suddenly recognised the song they were playing as one that Dad often sang, and I whispered out loud, 'Patience!' In the silence of the auditorium, my whisper reverberated around the whole theatre, and there was a loud ripple of laughter.

Those were very happy days for me at home with Mum before school beckoned. Like most married women with children at that time, she stayed at home to look after me; there was no thought of her going out to work and leaving me with a childminder or grandparents or in a nursery, unlike today. That sort of thing was practically unheard of. My memories of that time seem to be of eternally sunny days spent feeding the ducks on Clapton Pond or visiting 'the swings', which was a children's playground on the opposite side of Millfields, containing hobby horses, a slide, roundabout, sandpit, paddling pool and, of course, the eponymous swings. On other days, we would go out into the field behind our house for picnics, to which I would invariably bring Arabella, a large sit-on, push-along toy in the shape of a snail.

Arabella was my favourite toy as a toddler. She got her name from the giant snail that appeared in my favourite storybook of the time, *The Travels of Jeremy Jukes*. Among my other favourite books was Enid Blyton's *The Talking Teapot and Other Tales*, which featured a pixie called Dimble Dumble, Mr Tweaky and his magic pockets and the Chocolate Cock. For me, as for many children of the time, Enid Blyton provided the delightful stories and tales of well-behaved and naughty children, gnomes and fairies. In particular, I had many Noddy books and I loved hearing all about the scrapes he got into and his adventures with Big Ears and Mr Plod the Policeman.

My other great storybook 'hero' was Rupert Bear, who inhabited what to me was a truly magical and enchanting world. Many of his adventures took place in exotic lands with mermaids, pirates, jungles and mischievous imps far away from his home in the quintessential English village of Nutwood and in my imagination I was able to travel to these mysterious and glamorous lands with Rupert. His best friends, Bill Badger, Algy Pug and Edward Trunk, were my friends too. I was so immersed in Rupert's world that I didn't give him up until I went to grammar school, many years later.

All the books were printed in the same format, whereby the story was told in picture form with a simple two-line-per-image rhyming couplet verse immediately under the illustration and then as running prose at the foot of the page. I preferred the prose version because the verses did tend to be a bit repetitive and were not as interesting. 'Algy's looking very glum. What can be the matter with Rupert's chum?' is a typical refrain. One particular story began with the sentence 'Rupert looked out on the dismal scene' and was illustrated with Rupert looking out of his window as the rain poured down outside. This became a standard catchphrase in our family for years afterwards so that whenever it was raining outside one of us was bound to say, 'Rupert looked out on the dismal scene.'

When it did rain or we didn't go out, I would play happily with Mum or she would read to me, teaching me to read and write. The first words I ever wrote by myself were 'Tex The Cat', which I spelt out in brightly coloured plastic toy letters. Sometimes I wrote on the window with my finger after breathing on it, or I would write with crayons in an exercise book. I kept a box of toys especially for playing with outside, mostly containing cars, which I ran up and down the path next to our side door, as well as a spinning top. This was quite a large top, with the words to 'Sing a Song of Sixpence' written on it and illustrations from the nursery rhyme. It had to be pumped up and down a few times and then, when it was let go, it would spin with a loud hum. At the point of letting it go, I used to say, 'And the king said, "play my mu'ic"' – and it did.

On the occasions when I was playing happily on my own, Mum would get on with all the household jobs, like making the beds, which was a much more complex job than it is today, what with all the sheets and blankets, which had to be neatly folded and tucked in around the bed. She would do the washing up from breakfast, some washing and ironing, dusting, polishing both furniture and the cutlery, and in between all this she would be making lunch for us and dinner for the whole family when Dad and John came home from work and school.

The wireless was always on while Mum was doing her work round the house. Her favourite programmes were all on the Light Programme rather than the Home Service channel and included *Housewives' Choice*, *Mrs Dale's Diary*, *Music While You Work*, the organist Reginald Dixon broadcasting live from the Tower Ballroom, Blackpool and Mr 'Slow, slow, quick, quick, slow' himself, Victor Sylvester. His weekly worldwide request programme always fascinated me as he used to read out letters from places with very exotic-sounding names that I had never heard of and from countries now no longer in existence that were a real throwback to more colonial times, such as British Cameroons, British Togoland, Gold Coast, Northern Rhodesia and Nyasaland. Mum liked big band music, which was probably at the height of its popularity at that time. Her favourite musician was Mantovani, but she also liked Joe Loss, Oscar Rabin and Edmundo Ros. If there was no music on the wireless, she would sing away to herself, preferring the popular melodies of the day, especially Hoagy Carmichael's 'My Resistance is Low'.

Another of her jobs, particularly in winter, was to clean out the ashes from the fire grate and give it a good polish with Zebra black lead. This came in small, square black blocks in black and yellow striped paper. Along with everyone else in the prefabs, and probably across the road as well, our main source of heating was an open coal fire in the living room. The coal was delivered at regular intervals by the coalmen, who would have to hump one hundredweight sacks of coal up our path to the shed, where they would empty the coal out into the bin. Our coalmen were two brothers called J. & C. Edkins. They would arrive in their open-back lorry, which was piled high with sacks of coal. The brothers wore the clothes typical of a coalman of those days, a black waistcoat covering a red-and-white striped shirt with brown corduroy trousers. They also wore a leather cap on their heads, with a flap down the back to stop the coal getting inside their shirts. It was obvious that ours was not their first job of the day as their hands and faces were always covered in coal dust and looking as 'black as Newgate's Knocker', as Mum used to say. There was another rival firm, which also delivered locally, called Tilley & Sons. One day, while walking up Sewdley Street, we saw a sign in the window of one of the houses that read, 'Tilley, no coal today'. Although the occupants of this particular house were not close neighbours of ours, they were always known to us after this as 'Old Tilley No Coal'.

Mum used to take me shopping to our local market street, Chatsworth Road. Market day was Tuesday, with early closing on Thursday, something that was adhered to by every single shop and market stall. Once a week, we used to catch the no. 22 bus to Mare Street in the centre of Hackney, where we would call in on the Welfare place next to the Town Hall to get my weekly supply of free orange juice and Virol malt extract. Free 'Welfare Orange', as it was known, and malt had been introduced during the war years to make sure that children under five received their vitamins C and A. This was continued by the Labour Government as part of the new Welfare State being introduced under the Beveridge Report's proposals for 'cradle to the grave' social security and health provision. I loved the malt, which came in a big brown wide-mouthed jar. It was lovely gooey sticky stuff. I believe cod liver oil was offered as an alternative to malt, but I never had any as far as I can remember, or maybe I did and didn't like it so my parents settled for malt.

Mare Street was the main street in Hackney and, as well as the Welfare office, included among its buildings the Town Hall, the Central Library and the Hackney Empire, a still thriving example of a Music Hall theatre, as well as big shops such as Woolworths, Marks & Spencer and British Home Stores (BHS).

Being so young, I was rarely allowed out on my own, but one day I went for a walk into the field with Barry Tickton and Richard (Copper's son). I don't actually remember much about the walk itself but I can remember being sat on the table in the kitchen on my return and being given a good talking to. Apparently, what had happened was that Barry and Richard told Mum that they had taken me over to the far end of the field, near where the River Lea flowed. They lost me somehow and came running back, shouting to her that I had fallen in the river. Mum's face turned a ghostly white. She dropped everything and rushed out of the prefab, fearing the worst. Running into the field, she was yelling my name, barely able to control the tears. Suddenly, she saw a forlorn figure over the far side of the field, trudging slowly towards her. When she realised it was me, she ran and caught me, holding me to her so tightly I could hardly breathe. We made our way back to the prefab with her still clutching on to me, not daring to let me go. I couldn't understand why she was crying so much and wondered what had happened and if I'd done something wrong. It was only when we got back home and she sat me down on the kitchen table that she spoke to me for the first time, saying, 'Don't you ever go near that river again! I thought I'd lost you.' She then picked me up and gave me another big cuddle, far too relieved to see me in one piece to be cross with me. For my part, I couldn't really understand what all the fuss was about as I hadn't been near the river, let alone fallen into it. Why Barry and Richard told her that I had, I have no idea.

Although I hadn't been near the river this time, I did quite often go down there when I was older, either on my own or with friends. There was a big power station at the end of Millfields Road near the Marshes, which backed onto the river and was serviced by barges bringing the coal. The coal would be unloaded and lifted up into the power station by means of two large fixed-hoist cranes. Mostly the barges were pulled by tugs but some were still drawn by horses. It was fascinating seeing those barges make their way sedately up the river and then watching the coal being winched up.

In the evenings, I looked forward to Dad coming home from work and often used to look out the kitchen window to see if I could see him coming. If I did, I would run out to meet him. Once he was home and with tea out of the way, we would play games, usually paper games such as noughts and crosses and boxes, or simple card games like snap or 'Old Maid', or read until it was bedtime. In the summer, we might go outside and play a ball game, usually catch, though, after a hard day's work, Dad was usually too tired for anything too energetic. There were also a few occasions when he said, 'Let's go and see what we can find in Chatsworth Road,' and he would take me out to buy a small toy. I can remember him buying me two buses and a set of picture transfers on different occasions. Transfers were quite popular then. They came on sheets of paper, about a dozen on a sheet, and you'd cut out the one you wanted, soak it in water and the picture would float free of the paper. You could then stick it down in a book or on a toy as a decoration.

We owned a cat that was almost totally black, with a large white spot under his chin, so I called him Spot (well, I *was* only four years old). He never grew much bigger than a large kitten and he was my companion until long after we had moved away from Hackney. I have had a number of cats since Spot and all of them have been quite fussy about which tinned food they eat. It was just as well Spot wasn't, as Kit-e-Kat was the only brand available then. When it was time to feed him, we put his plate on a sheet of newspaper on the floor. The newspaper was kept in one of the drawers in the kitchen cabinet and, whenever he went into the kitchen, Spot would jump up to the drawers to let you know it was time for food.

He went missing one day and, despite searching all of his regular haunts, we couldn't find him anywhere. The days passed into weeks, the weeks into months and there was no sign of him anywhere. Heartbroken, we gave him up for lost. Then, one day, we heard a faint miaowing outside the side door and, when we opened it, there he was. He presented a very sorry sight. He was dirty, sore, dishevelled, bruised and with a torn ear. We took him straight to the vet, who told us he would recover if looked after and not allowed out for a few days. That cat became the most looked-after cat of all time and within a week or so was back to his old self. We never did find out what had happened to him, though.

As well as Spot, we also kept a budgerigar called Bluey (another one of Dad's little jokes as he was actually green!) and a couple of tortoises, known as Shadwell and Wapping, in the back garden. I'm afraid we weren't very good at helping the tortoises hibernate and both of them died in the winter. We also lost the budgerigar when it flew out of the door. Dad had taken it out of the cage in the kitchen to clean it out, as he had done many previous times. As usual, it was allowed to fly freely around until it was time to put it back. On this particular occasion, there was a knock at the side door and outside was a group of kids, asking if they could get their ball back as they had kicked it over into our garden. Because we lived on a field, this was a frequent request. Dad's response was always, 'You can get it this time, but, if it comes over again, you're not getting it back.' Of course, they always did get it back, however many times it came over. It was while he was making his standard reply that the budgerigar saw his chance for freedom and flew out the open door, never to be seen again.

The kitchen cabinet where we kept the newspaper was also home to the shilling jar – an old malt jar – for the electric meter. We tried to remember to put a shilling in before the electric ran out but very often forgot, so quite frequently we would be watching television when suddenly it, and all the lights, would go off. One of us then had to grope our way through the dark to find the shilling jar and then the electricity meter, which was in the hallway on the other side of the house. Whenever we got a shilling in change, it would go in the jar – I don't think we ever actually spent a shilling piece in the shops.

Every quarter, the electricity man would come and empty our meter. He would give us a small rebate and we'd put the shillings back in the jar. Once, we completely ran out of shillings when the electricity went out. The only shilling in the house was an eighteenth-century George III shilling, which Dad had managed to get hold of somewhere. Reluctantly, he put this in the meter but told Mum to make sure when the electricity man came to get this one back in the rebate. Fortunately, it was rebated safely.

While I was enjoying what can only be described as an idyllic childhood in my prefab on the field, I was blissfully unaware of the major trauma my parents were going through. John had passed his 11-plus exam with such a high mark that he was offered the chance of going to public school, either Christ's Hospital, Westminster or Bancroft's, on a scholarship. John's headmaster, Mr Foreman, advised my parents that, of the three, Christ's Hospital near Horsham in Sussex would be the best bet. Mum and Dad didn't want him to leave to go to a boarding school and couldn't understand why a child should be removed from the security of his family at the very young age of eleven. However, they also realised that this would be a wonderful opportunity for him and, after much agonising and discussions with John, it was decided he would fill in the application form for Christ's Hospital. Shortly afterwards, he was asked to sit an entrance exam. Dad took him up to a place in Holborn, where he underwent a medical, an interview and a written exam. When he came out, Dad asked him what sort of questions he'd had to answer.

John said, 'How many 2½d stamps can you buy for a £1 was one of them.'

Dad pulled a face and said, 'Did you know?'

John replied, 'Of course, ninety-six.'

Dad knew then that he was going to lose his elder son to a boarding school in Sussex. Shortly afterwards, a letter came from the school confirming his place and instructions on when and how to get there. He was to go to Victoria station on the appointed day and join up with the other masters and boys on the train to Horsham.

When the day came, there was hardly a dry eye in the house – apart from mine, as I had no idea what was going on. He took his leave of Mum at the prefab and Dad accompanied him to Victoria station on the 38 bus. Grasping his small attaché case in his hand, John made his way to the appointed platform and was caught up in a vast milling crowd of old hands and new boys, many of the latter in tears, along with their parents. John joined his group and Dad hung around, waiting for the inevitable guard's whistle. It came all too soon and the train slowly but surely chugged out of the station. Dad waited until the train finally disappeared from sight then made his way back to the bus stop with a very empty feeling inside. It was the end of an era. In fact, more so than anyone imagined at the time as, apart from holidays, John never again lived at home, eventually going straight on to university and then to work, sharing a flat with a friend before getting married.

Bad as this was for my parents, the trauma wasn't over yet. When John came home for the Christmas holidays, he told them he didn't want to go back and didn't like it at school. Mum would have pulled him out there and then, but, in spite of wanting nothing better than to have John back home, Dad knew that this was a wonderful opportunity for him and felt it was essential he should see it through. Two wretched people left the prefab on a bleak January morning to catch the bus to Victoria. In fact, it turned out that an older boy was bullying John and this was the main cause of his unhappiness. A bad enough thing normally, but being on your own and miles away from your loved ones must have made it a hundred times worse. When the problem was eventually sorted out, John took to life at Christ's Hospital with great relish and never looked back.

It wasn't long before I too was to experience a mini-trauma of my own when I suddenly found myself parted from Mum and plonked in front of a desk in a classroom with about thirty other children. A woman was introduced to us as Miss Leach who, apparently, was to be my teacher, whatever that was.

Yes, schooldays had arrived. On the morning they did, I was blissfully unaware of the life-changing event about to overwhelm me. That fateful day, Mum got me ready and took me out (I suppose I thought we were going shopping or something). Instead, we entered this big building with hundreds of other children, went into a large room where I was placed behind a desk while Mum stood by the door, waving… and then left. I had never been parted from her before so I just leaned forward, put my head in my hands and sobbed. I'm sure it must have been just as hard – if not harder – for Mum to leave me in that state.

At lunchtime, when she came to pick me up, I'm sure she must have been very worried about what she would find and how I was bearing up but she was in for a bit of a shock as I told her I couldn't wait to return to school. Miss Leach was reading us a story and I was eager to get back to hear the rest of it!

And so, with school now about to play a major role in my everyday life, a whole new era of growing up in London's East End in the 1950s and 1960s began.

CHAPTER TWO

MARBLES, CONKERS AND 'BASH-UPS'

A normal school day usually started with Mum waking me up. Getting out of bed could be a real chore in the winter. Without central heating and with our main source of warmth just the open coal fire in the living room, it could be, and usually was, freezing cold. Many times I would get up and see the window covered with Jack Frost's patterns expertly drawn all over the inside of the bedroom window. After shivering my way through the morning ablutions, it was with a great sense of relief that I went into the living room to warm myself up before the roaring coal fire. Then it was into the kitchen for some breakfast. This was usually cereal: Weetabix, Rice Krispies and Shredded Wheat were my favourites. Mum always made them with warm milk and it wasn't until many years later that I realised most people had cold milk on their breakfast cereal.

At that time there wasn't the great variety of cereal that there is now and, when a new one hit the market in 1953, Mum gave it to me to try out. I took one mouthful and decided that I didn't like Shreddies at all! I don't know what happened to the rest of the box, but I certainly couldn't eat any more. At the time many different small toys were given away inside cereal packets. About a year later, Shreddies were offering some glow-in-the-dark stickers that I thought looked really good so I persuaded Mum to buy another packet with the argument that perhaps I might like them now. I still only got as far as the first mouthful, but at least I had some excellent stickers.

Mum always took me to infants' school. It was about a seven-minute walk if you crossed the bomb site in Chatsworth Road, a little bit longer if you went round it (this was the same bomb site where John had injured his leg just before I was born). The site, a whole block of about ten former shops between Elderfield Road and Lockhurst Street, was left derelict well into the 1950s and was a real adventure ground for children as we used to climb about over the rubble and broken glass, looking for anything that might be valuable or just playing in the ruins. There was no thought of it being cordoned off as it surely would be today; it was just left open. The fact that it was actually quite dangerous while at the same time a magnet to young children never seemed to occur to anyone.

The school I went to was Rushmore Road Primary School. Our school colours were maroon and grey and I proudly wore my cap, blazer, school tie and socks. My shirt was white in warm weather and grey in cold weather; I wore grey flannel shorts whatever the weather.

School introduced me to a whole new set of people, but

Barry Tickton, whom I already knew, took me under his wing to explain a few things about life at school and, indeed, life generally. Barry's first piece of advice was to avoid the large dogs called 'sarnations' as they would bite you if you got too close. His second was to avoid old men as they would 'pinch' you and run off with you. For some time, I was very wary of the old boys who used to sit on the park benches in Millfields, puffing away at their pipes, taking snuff and chatting. As I passed them by, keeping my distance as much as possible, I often wondered where it was they would take you after they'd pinched you. Fortunately, we had neither 'sarnations' nor old men at Rushmore Road school so I felt pretty safe once inside.

My first teacher was Miss Leach. Mysteriously, at the beginning of the second term, she became Mrs Farioni. We all speculated on this change of name with some wild imaginings but I don't think any of us hit on the truth that she had got married to Mr Farioni during the holiday. Being a spy or a criminal wanted by the police seemed a much more plausible and interesting reason to change your name.

The Headmistress was Miss Taylor. On our second day at school, she came round to introduce herself and to find out our names. I sat next to a boy called Freddy Loosey, and when Miss Taylor asked his name he, of course, said, 'Freddy Loosey.' Miss Taylor put on a very serious face and said, 'Well, you'd better tighten yourself up then.' For some reason I thought this was really funny and laughed out loud. Freddy scowled at me.

I had two more teachers in the Infants' School, Mrs Raymond and Miss Corbett. Miss Corbett had grey hair and seemed to me to be at least a hundred years old. Sometimes we had to take our exercise books out to the front and stand by her at the desk while she went through our work. I always hated it when her hair touched my face as it seemed to sting; I don't know what she put on it.

Of course, it was at school that we learnt about reading, writing and doing sums, though I could already do a bit of each before ever going to school, thanks to my parents. In our first year, we wrote on individual blackboards with a chalk but progressed to small books and pencils as we moved up the school. Although we did our three Rs through most of the week, it wasn't all hard work. Miss Leach/Mrs Farioni sometimes used to take us out into the playground to play games with us, the most popular being 'What's the time, Mr Wolf?' and 'The Farmer's in his Den':

> The Farmer's in his den,
> The Farmer's in his den,
> E I de addy oh,
> The Farmer's in his den.

We never played these games with Mrs Raymond or Miss Corbett but Friday afternoon was always set aside for play, when we were allowed to bring in a toy from home.

I have two outstanding personal memories of Infants' School. The first was when HM the Queen and Prince Philip undertook a six-month tour of the Commonwealth, starting in late 1953 after the Coronation. One morning in Assembly with the whole school present, Miss Taylor asked us if we knew where the Queen was at that moment. I was the only child in the whole school to put his hand up. 'She's crossing the Tasmanian Sea,' I said. I think I must have heard this on the wireless before I left for school that morning, but, anyway, it was the correct answer and Miss Taylor was suitably impressed with my general knowledge. (This must have been the start of my quiz career that was to see me defeat C.J. in my head-to-head challenge on BBC TV's *Eggheads* in 2007 and win £10,000 on ITV's *Tipping Point* in 2013!)

The second was when Miss Taylor was casting for the school's Christmas play. All I can remember about the play now is that it starred three pixies called Hop, Lol and Gig, who came across a little girl lost in the woods. The first line was spoken by Hop, who said, 'Hello, little girl.' I was given the part of Hop because I was the only boy in the school who could pronounce girl as it was written. Everyone else said, ''ello, little gel,' except Bob Marriott, who was keen to show that he had learnt not to say 'gel' and said, 'Hello, little gol,' instead.

The Junior School was across the road from the Infants' School and took up the whole block on Chatsworth Road between Rushmore Road and Rushmore Crescent. Whereas the Infants' School was very straightforward, with all the classrooms being situated off the main hall, the Junior School was a maze of corridors, stairs and rooms that took me the four years I was there to get to know my way round. There were some strange doors that just seemed to lead nowhere and stairs you could see from the outside but couldn't find on the inside; also a staircase with a door halfway up it, which took you on to an entirely different staircase, leading to the library. Hogwarts could well have been modelled on Rushmore Road Junior School.

My first class was 1A, which was on the ground floor and reached through a tunnel that led off the playground and into a small corridor, off which were three classrooms: one on the left, 4A, and two on the right, 1A and 1B. The hall was also off this corridor to the right, while the dining hall was off to the left. My teacher was Mr Moore. He was quite a pleasant sort, though he did have his off days when no one could do anything right, but these were fortunately quite rare. He was probably in his late twenties, though he seemed very old to me, as did all the teachers. Whereas in the Infants' School we mainly learnt the three Rs, in the Junior School we now began to learn other subjects such as history, geography and nature study, all of which I found infinitely more interesting than English and arithmetic.

The normal school day was broken into several lessons, all of them, with the exception of music, taken by Mr Moore. We sat in blocks of six, with our desks pushed together. Our desks had a circular hole in the top at the front made for a porcelain inkwell as we were now expected to use pen and ink. We were all issued with a standard pen made up of a yellow wooden shaft with a small nib on the end. There was no ink reservoir, so we had to continually dip the nib into the inkwell, scratch out a few words and dip in again. The first thing we did with these pens was to learn 'joined-up' writing.

Classes were streamed by ability and, even within our class, Mr Moore streamed us by putting the top performers together on one table and so on down to the bottom end. The desks were arranged so that the top table was in the back right of the class and the bottom table at the lower left. There were three of us who were always on the top table: my friend Andy Shalders, Margaret Smith and me (the other occupants varied over the course of the four years). The only problem with being on the top table at the back of the class was that from about the age of ten onwards I couldn't see the blackboard! I didn't say anything about it as I thought it was normal and that no one else could see it from that distance. However, it was the first sign that I was actually short-sighted. Eventually, at the age of eleven, I started wearing glasses and things improved.

Looking back on it, I am sure that it was here that I first developed my love of history, which is something that has defined my whole life and career ever since. It was the Ancient Egyptians that did it. I found stories about mummies and pharaohs absolutely enthralling. Ancient Egypt was a completely different world, and as fascinating to me as any alien planet. One of the school history books described the life of the Ancient Egyptians through the eyes of a seven-year-old boy of the time and I was able to identify with him completely as I became fully absorbed in his world.

As well as these more academic subjects, we also had time for the arts, music and painting. Not that my painting was anything to write home about as I could never get the hang of drawing a human body properly and simply drew a big round circle for the body, a smaller one for the head just stuck on top (no neck) and four limbs sticking out at forty-five-degree angles. We used to do painting once a week when some of the better artists were chosen to paint a big picture that would be stuck up on the wall. I think in the four years I was in Junior School I was only once asked to paint a big picture and this was mainly because I had written a good story and Mr Moore thought I should have the chance of illustrating it. I seem to recall the picture was of a large green fire-breathing dragon, which had a big round circle for the body, a smaller one for the head, etc., etc.

At the end of playtime, the teacher on playground duty blew a whistle and we all had to line up in our classes – no talking – to wait for the signal to move off to our class. A few weeks after I started Junior School, we were lining up in the playground when Mr Brown, an ancient teacher with snow-white hair, appeared and led us up the stairs to a different classroom. 'He's made a mistake, he thinks our classroom is upstairs,' I thought to myself. However, I soon discovered he wasn't wrong as he took us into the music room; this was a room with a stepped floor. At the front of the room was a piano, at which Mr Brown sat, while the rest of us sat on the steps. His first act was to ask all the boys to sing a few notes individually. After listening, he proclaimed us either a 'singer' or a 'growler'. I was designated a growler and had to sit with my fellow growlers on the front step. Growlers were never given a second chance, so I remained one all my Junior School life and was mostly ignored by Mr Brown as he felt we had no chance of ever being able to sing properly.

Most of our music lessons consisted of Mr Brown teaching us to sing Olde English folk songs such as 'Barbara Allen', 'Sir Eglamore' and 'The British Grenadiers'. One of the first songs he taught us was 'The Owl', with words by Alfred, Lord Tennyson, which had the refrain: 'Alone and warming his five wits, The white owl in the belfry sits.' After we'd practised it a few times, Mr Brown felt that we were ready to sing it all the way through. As he struck the first chord on the piano, the boy sitting next to me, David Burt, whispered in my ear, 'Come closer to me and listen to what I sing.' He then sang his own adjustment to the refrain, 'Alone and warming his five tits, The white owl in the belfry sits.' He thought this was hilarious, but, having led a sheltered life myself, I didn't understand what was so funny.

Mr Brown was very much an old-style teacher. He had been at Rushmore many years and was well known to my brother, who had left Rushmore Junior School three years earlier. In fact, my family all knew about Mr Brown because John had told us a story about him, some years previously. Apparently, one morning, just before school was due to start, one of the boys walked out of the playground intending to go to Willis's sweet shop across the road. Mr Brown saw him leave and followed him. Just outside the school gate, he put his fingers down the back of the boy's blazer and hauled him back, saying, 'Where are you going, cre-a-ture? Get back here!' As befitted a teacher of the old school, Mr Brown was not above doling out corporal punishment on a frequent basis, most often a clip round the ear or a ruler across the knuckles. Sometimes, if it was serious enough, he would send the miscreant to the Headmaster to be caned and the misdeed written in the dreaded punishment book.

Of course, such behaviour would not be tolerated these days, but even worse was the game Mr Brown recommended we could play when we were outside school. He told us that when crossing the road we should wait until a car was fairly near and then run across in front of it. We could earn two points if it was really close and one point if it was not so close. Just writing this now makes me shudder to think a) what would have happened if there'd been an accident while we were playing this, and b) what would happen to him, had he said this to a class now. Mainly because of the fact he quite often resorted to corporal punishment, Mr Brown was feared and hated by all the pupils. Everyone avoided him if they could.

Mr Moore was not nearly so keen on corporal punishment as Mr Brown was, although he wasn't entirely opposed to using it. I don't remember anyone ever being sent to the Headmaster and his worst action was a sharp smack on the bottom or on the legs. But he only did this to boys; he wouldn't touch girls. One day I heard him telling off one of the girls in our class for something she had done and he said to her, 'If you were a boy, I'd give you a smack.' This struck me as most unfair. Why should girls be able to get away with doing what they liked without fear of reprisal whereas boys couldn't?

The other 'old timer' at the school was Mr Bristow, who had been John's class teacher. Now retired, he came back every now and then to help out. He was quite a decent old boy and not like Mr Brown, whom everyone hated. The only other teacher who had been at Rushmore in John's time was the Headmaster, Mr 'Fatty' Foreman. He, too, was a decent sort, though he never saw much of us as he mostly stayed in his office. I don't remember him ever doing any actual teaching.

Most of the other teachers were fairly young like Mr Moore. The two I saw most were Mr Wills and Mr Evans. Mr Wills taught the 'B' stream and was responsible for destroying my illusion that teachers knew everything. One day, when I was about nine years old, he came into our classroom and said loudly to Mr Moore, 'What's the speed of light? Someone's just asked me and I can't remember.' I couldn't believe it, a teacher not knowing something! Impossible. Even with Mr Moore's immediate response, '186,000 miles per second,' I was still left in a state of shock that Mr Wills didn't know this.

Mr Evans was my favourite teacher. The sporty one, he did all the things we liked. He took us for games and also held drama classes after school, which I loved. His only failing was not recognising in me the great footballer I considered myself to be, but I put this down to the fact that the school employed one of the parents, Mr Hart, as an outside coach. I played at centre-half, which, sadly, was the favoured position of Mr Hart's son, John. Guess who he chose for the school team?

We got on better with cricket, though here again I never quite made the team except on one occasion when I came on as a substitute. However, I did manage to become the school's official scorer, so I went to every match. In those days, the school cricket team took part in a properly structured league with all the other local primary schools. Our home ground was on North Millfields, next to the children's playground. I became scorer by accident when the boy who was doing it was off sick one day. Mr Evans asked me if I'd like to do it. As it happened, I had a cold myself that day, and my parents had told me to come straight home after school. To make matters worse, the sky was very dark, threatening an impending storm; so, naturally, I said yes. Bob Marriott, who lived near me and passed my prefab on his way home, asked if he should tell my parents I would be late. I don't know why but I told him not to tell them. So off I went to score my first match as Rushmore's official scorer. The rain held off for most of the match but then started to pour down and I faced the walk home with my cold in the pouring rain. When I got home, I explained where I'd been. Immediately they forgot their worries about what might have happened to me: Dad, who loved cricket, was so proud of me becoming the official scorer that was all he could talk about.

That first time I scored was also the first time I heard the same joke that every opposition scorer made. When we arrived, the two scorers got together to let the other know the names of his team members. Our opening bat was Alan Oakley, but we always just gave initials, so it was A. Oakley. I don't think there was one boy who didn't make some joke to the effect that we had Annie Oakley opening our batting and think it was a) highly amusing and b) original. I continued as Rushmore's official scorer until I left school.

The only sporting event I didn't enjoy with Mr Evans was swimming. On Friday afternoons, he took our class to Hackney Baths in Lower Clapton Road but he never really bothered to teach us how to swim. Because I couldn't swim, he used to leave me, along with the other non-swimmers, in the shallow end just playing around, while he concentrated on the swimmers and helping them get their 50- and 100-yards certificates. For me, the best part of the afternoon was going into the sweet shop next door to the baths to buy a piece of honeycomb, which I took home to share with Mum. She looked forward to this treat as much as I did. My friends Andy and Terry always came back with me and we'd sit down to watch *Jungle Jim*, starring former Olympic swimming champion Johnny Weissmuller, on television.

A good swimmer herself, Mum was disappointed by my lack of progress so she wrote a letter to the school, telling them that she was not going to let me go to any more swimming lessons and she would teach me herself. It never struck me as strange at the time but just writing this makes me wonder why the school agreed to this. However, agree they did and once under Mum's tuition I quickly learnt the rudiments of the breaststroke. My big breakthrough came one summer when we were on holiday and, on my return to school, I was allowed back to Mr Evans and his lessons. I joined the swimmers and quickly gained my 50-yards certificate. However, I have to say to this day I have never really been that keen on swimming.

Apart from sport, Mr Evans' other contribution to the life of the school was drama. As well as organising the annual Christmas play, he also ran a voluntary drama class after school. He taught me a lot about theatre techniques, both acting and technical. The best acting tip I can remember was his telling us that comedy acting was best done seriously. He got about seven or eight of us to stand in line and asked how we would march if he told us to make it funny. Some of the boys started doing exaggerated movements and making wild gestures as they were marching. He stopped us and got us to line up again, this time behind each other but as close as we could get, before saying, 'Turn left and march in line without trying to be funny.' The result was hilarious as we marched in step so close together, trying not to bump into each other. It looked really comical but we were trying to do it seriously without the exaggeration and silly gestures. Lesson learnt.

Mr Evans was also the first person in authority I came across who didn't try to persuade us that the new musical craze for rock'n'roll was rubbish. Everyone else, parents and teachers and so on, thought it was a bad influence and did all they could to dissuade us from listening to it. But Mr Evans actually brought in records to the after-school classes and got us to loosen up by doing a bit of jiving. His favourite for getting us going was the theme from *The Man with the Golden Arm*, which in itself was a bit controversial as the film, released in 1955, was one of the first to deal with drug addiction, though, of course, none of us knew anything about this at the time.

With the arrival of rock'n'roll, youngsters had their own music for the first time; it was music generally reviled by adults, and it was that which made it so attractive... well, that and the excitement of the music itself, of course. Until then, popular music could be and was enjoyed by all generations. The popular singers were mainly crooners such as Bing Crosby, Frank Sinatra and Perry Como. But the first sign of youngster-specific music came when Johnnie Ray hit the big time with songs like 'Cry', 'The Little White Cloud That Cried' and 'Such a Night'. Though not full-blown rock'n'roll by any means, Ray attracted a younger audience with his exaggerated move-ments and voice intonation, but it was when Bill Haley & His Comets hit the scene that young people (the word 'teenager' was still a new word in those days) discovered they had music of their very own that was hated by their parents and other authority figures. There was outrage in Hackney when our nearest cinema, The Castle in Brooksby's Walk, showed *Rock Around the Clock* and teenagers actually got up out of their seats and danced in the aisles.

A new era had begun. And things got better (or worse, according to your point of view) when Elvis Presley arrived on the scene. His singing was electrifying, but what the older generation found really offensive were his overtly sexual dance moves that earned him the nickname of 'Elvis the Pelvis'. In America, after a show in Wisconsin, the local Catholic Church sent an urgent message to the FBI director J. Edgar Hoover warning that 'Presley is a definite danger to the security of the United States. … [His] actions and motions were such as to rouse the sexual passions of teenaged youth. …' American youth, meanwhile, took a different view. After the show, more than a thousand teenagers tried to get into Presley's room at the auditorium. Youth culture had arrived and led to a whole new way of life, not just in music but in everything, especially clothes.

Until the 1950s, youngsters followed their parents' fashions, but, with the birth of rock'n'roll, this changed forever. Teenagers were no longer younger copies of their parents, but became people in their own right with their own fashions, language and identity, of which the Teddy Boys were the most extreme example. At school, the first signs of this came when many of the boys stopped wearing school uniform. It had never actually been compulsory, although most wore it but in the late 1950s there was a big fashion for leather jackets, something our parents would never dream of wearing. Most boys had black jackets, a few had red ones, but even then, although I wanted to take part in this rebellion, I still wanted to show my individuality and so I persuaded Mum and Dad to buy me a green leather jacket. I was the only boy at school to have a green one.

Milk bars with jukeboxes also arrived as places where teenagers could hang out on their own and where kids were encouraged to listen to and even make their own music, skiffle. Hackney had its very own milk bar in Mare Street, where you could also buy that other modern innovation: espresso coffee straight from Italy. To see the shiny new Gaggia Espresso Machine spluttering away amid clouds of steam and spilling out its glamorous new drink was a wonderful and liberating experience, one that belonged exclusively to the young. Not only was skiffle played on the jukebox but groups of kids would give impromptu performances too.

British skiffle music was a homegrown development of American rock'n'roll that shot to prominence following the release of Lonnie Donegan's hit record 'Rock Island Line' in 1956. Its main appeal was that it was cheap to imitate and therefore popular among the young, who could improvise or build their own instruments at little or no cost. Not only was skiffle a different type of music, one we could call our own, but it was also easy to have a go. No need for expensive instruments, just get a secondhand beat-up guitar or, if you couldn't afford that, you could join in with your mum's washboard or a large box with a string attached for a bass. And, better still, you didn't even have to be American. Whereas rock stars like Elvis Presley and Chuck Berry were looked on as superstars that we could never aspire to be, the leading skiffle proponents were local working-class kids like ourselves. Along with Lonnie Donegan, other homegrown acts such as The Vipers and Tommy Steele burst onto the scene, encouraging British kids like me to have a go. When I was ten years old, there was talk of some of us in our class forming a homemade skiffle group. I auditioned in front of the boy who decided he'd be the group leader, giving a full rendition of 'Cumberland Gap'. I thought I'd performed pretty well, but his only comment was, 'You need to move your hips more.' And so, at the tender age of ten, that was the end of my career as a rock star. Mind you, the group never formed anyway.

My parents and grandparents were forever grumbling about rock'n'roll. Although not quite a teenager yet myself, I wanted to watch television programmes like *6:5 Special* and *Oh Boy!* just coming on to BBC television in the late 1950s to cater for this new young audience but Dad wouldn't hear of it. 'That music is rubbish,' he used to complain. 'It'll never last like the old songs.' And he'd quickly turn over to ITV, much to my great disappointment. In the mid-1950s, many Victorian and Edwardian Music Hall songs were still well known. We are now about as far away from the mid-1950s as they were from the late Victorian and Edwardian period so I think it's safe to say we can dismiss the theory that rock'n'roll singers and songs will never last as long! I mean, whatever happened to Cliff Richard anyway?

It was with the start of Junior School that I began to make some real friends with whom I played outside of school. In particular, there were Andy Shalders, Bob Marriott, Peter Hannaford, John Walker, Howard Bradbury and Terry Gregory. We formed a group – I think it would be wrong to say a gang – and stuck together for the whole of the time we were in Junior School. Of these boys, my best friend was Andy, a slightly tubby boy, who, like me, was very keen on playing and watching sports. His father managed a grocer's shop in Chatsworth Road and, although it wasn't one we frequented as shoppers, I did go round there quite a lot to play with Andy. There was one occasion when I was there alone in the shop after he had gone off to the toilet. For some reason I decided to see how sharp the bacon slicer was. I can confirm that it was very sharp indeed – I just touched it and it almost sliced my finger off! There was blood everywhere. I ran home as fast as I could. Fortunately, it looked worse than it was and Mum was able to sort everything out with an Elastoplast. Andy must have wondered what had happened when he came back from the loo and saw a trail of blood on the floor but no sign of me.

Bob Marriott lived closest to me. He had quite striking ginger hair and lived on the top floor of a terraced house in Chippendale Street. The bottom floor was occupied by the owner, Mrs Percy, a widowed woman in her eighties. She had snow-white hair and was always dressed completely in black from head to toe as though in perpetual mourning. I had strict instructions to knock on the door twice if I wanted to see Bob as one knock was for Mrs Percy and she wasn't happy if a caller knocked once and made her come to the door and then it turned out to be for upstairs. Bob said when that happened she complained to his parents and wouldn't let him forget it for days afterwards. His father was in the wood trade like my dad and also worked in Shoreditch. Bob was the only friend I had whose parents actually owned a car, a Ford Zephyr, which enabled them to go off to such exotic locations as Cornwall for their holidays.

I often walked back from school with Terry Gregory as he had to pass my house on his way home and, whereas conversations with most of my friends revolved around sport, Terry and I used to discuss some deep scientific conundrums such as when did time start and did the Universe come to an end. It was all very deep stuff for Junior School children. Terry lives in Australia these days but I am still in touch with him and even visited him a few years ago.

Peter Hannaford was the boy who introduced us all to the wonders of the female form. He had discovered a newsagent's shop in Lower Clapton Road that displayed copies of *H&E* (*Health & Efficiency*) in their front window and took us up there one day after school. So there we were, seven ten-year-olds stood gazing in the window at the front covers of these magazines for some minutes. I'm not sure what we all made of the experience other than somehow knowing we were doing something a bit rude that our parents and teachers wouldn't approve of and that this was our little collective secret. I don't think actually looking at bare female breasts in itself really did anything for us at that age. It was more the fact of doing something a bit naughty that we knew we shouldn't be doing that was the thrill. It also enhanced Peter's reputation as a grown-up 'man of the world'.

Johnnie Walker was a very quiet lad and, although he enjoyed playing football and cricket with us, he always seemed happier when we decided to settle for a board game or a game of marbles – something less energetic anyway.

As with all the others, I got on well with Howard Bradbury, but he was also a rival of mine when it came to running. We were both fast runners and often raced each other on the fields after school and in the holidays. But the real test came with the School Sports Day every year. This took place on Millfields at the back of my house so I was always on home ground. There were four houses at school, Red, Yellow, Green and Blue, and we used to compete against each other in various events such as running, jumping and throwing to win individual prizes and the overall team prize. Those were the days when there was proper competitive sport in schools, none of this non-competitive stuff they have these days to spare the losers' feelings. As a fast sprinter, I was always entered into the 50 Yards for my team, the Reds. In each of the four years I was in Junior School, the 50 Yards came down to a race between Howard, who was in the Blue Team, Patrick McConnell, Yellow, and David Brown and me for the Reds. We were the first four every year. Patrick was always the one to beat and he won the race three times, his only loss being to David. Second, third and fourth varied and I did manage second on a couple of occasions. Even if I couldn't win, it always gave me a great sense of satisfaction to be able to beat Howard.

The seven of us used to play together at playtime, not without any others, but always together. The games we used to play included football, Cowboys and Indians and 'War'. The Junior School playground was divided into two sections, one for the boys and one for the girls, as presumably it was felt that the boys would play too rough for the girls. The girls' playground was behind a wall but there was an opening through which we could see them playing.

Mostly we weren't interested in what they were doing as it seemed to consist mainly of 'cissy' skipping games or Hopscotch. But sometimes they played at handstands against the wall, and being upside down, of course, meant that their dresses dropped down over their heads to expose their knickers. When this happened there would usually be a crowd, particularly of the older boys, round the opening, trying to get a look. Why they bothered to do this was a bit of a mystery to me as we used to do P.E. together in our normal mixed class and saw the girls in their vests and knickers then anyway.

Meanwhile, back in the boys' playground, at the beginning of playtime, two boys would quite often get together, link arms and walk round the playground chanting rhythmically, 'Who wants to play Cowboys and Indians?' (Or whatever it was they wanted to play.) If you wanted to play, you'd link arms and this would go on until there were enough boys linked up to make a decent game. Sometimes there could be as many as ten or twelve boys walking through the playground in a line, chanting. The game would then commence. If it was Cowboys and Indians, you would be given the choice of which side you wanted to be on but as nearly everyone wanted to be a cowboy there was always a certain amount of coercion on the part of bigger and stronger boys to make sure others 'volunteered' to be Indians. The game then proceeded with everyone using their fingers as guns, pointing the index and middle fingers and making a shooting noise, which was a sort of a guttural 'K-K' sound. One of our teachers once said to us, 'Why don't you say "bang" instead of making that funny noise?' We thought this was a remarkably silly thing to say as everyone knew that guns went K-K, not bang. When you fired at someone, they were supposed to die, but the act of shooting at them was nearly always the cause of an argument: 'You're dead!', 'No, I'm not, you missed!', 'No, I didn't!' and 'Anyway, I shot you first!' Sometimes this argument could actually lead to real blows with fists, though most times it was settled in a reasonably amicable manner, i.e. the bigger boy would get his own way. If you were shot, you were dead until one of your side released you by touching you and you came back to life.

War, of course, was a similar game, only fought between the English and the Germans. Although we were all born after the Second World War, its legacy still played a big part in our lives. When I started at school, it had been over for only seven years and some rationing was still in force. All our parents had lived through the nightmare, with many of our fathers having seen active service somewhere and with their own exciting tales to tell. Indeed, many of us had older siblings who had been born during the War and, rightly or wrongly, there was still an intense feeling of animosity towards Germans generally. No one seemed to separate Germans from Nazis – as far as the generation that had come through the War was concerned, they were the same thing.

This feeling of intense hatred towards the Germans led to a real crisis of conscience for Dad in 1957 as, during the summer holidays, John, who was studying French and German at A-level, took part in an exchange programme, which meant his staying with a German family for two weeks and, horror of horrors, a German student, Michael Thermann, staying with us. For John's sake, Dad did his best not to let his discomfort show, but he barely said two words to Michael for the entire fortnight that he was with us. Michael did amuse us, though, because whenever we gave him an apple he used to eat the lot, stalk, core, pips, everything, and when he had fish he would eat the bones. He never left anything. We didn't know whether this was normal German behaviour, whether he was being polite in not wanting to leave anything or whether he was just so afraid of my dad that he didn't dare leave anything.

This feeling of animosity rubbed off on us, of course, though I like to think that as my generation grew up we realised that Germans and Nazis were far from the same thing. But when we played those games, it was all very simple: the English were the 'goodies' and the Germans were the 'baddies'. Absolutely nobody wanted to be a German, but someone had to be for everyone to play the game, so the same rules applied as finding Indians for the Cowboys and Indians games. As well as playing War outside, most boys would draw war pictures in the classroom, either in actual art lessons or when there was a bit of spare time. The most popular picture was of a British plane dropping bombs on a German battleship; it made for an exciting image. All of these feelings about the War and Germans were reinforced by much of the popular culture of the time since films, books, comics, songs and television all owed much to this legacy. There were numerous television programmes presented by generals like Field Marshal Viscount Montgomery and Lieutenant-General Sir Brian Horrocks, and classic films such as *The Dam Busters* and *Reach for the Sky* were staples of 1950s cinema.

Another reminder of the war years was the fact that every now and then in the early fifties the army would hold exercises on Hackney Marshes, during which they would send up barrage balloons. As soon as word got round that this was happening, all the boys in the neighbourhood got there as fast as they could. To us, it was very exciting but to our parents I expect it was just another reminder of days they'd rather forget.

Sometimes the act of two boys linking arms was an end in itself when it was done behind their backs as these would become 'bash-ups' and the boys themselves would run round into everyone they could, trying to knock them over. In self-defence you and a friend would form a bash-up of your own. This game was very much frowned upon by the teachers, who stopped it whenever they saw it happening.

There were a number of quieter games as well that seemed to appear seasonally. These were games like conkers, marbles, gobs and ciggies. There was, of course, a good reason why conkers should be seasonal, but why the others came and went on regular cycles I'm not really sure. Getting hold of conkers wasn't that difficult as there were a few horse chestnut trees around Millfields. The trick was to pick the best ones – usually small hard ones – soak them in vinegar and then bake them for no longer than two minutes. This, so it was said, would make them really hard and almost unbreakable.

Marbles were always made of glass and some had quite intricate coloured patterns inside. There were a number of different games we would play with marbles; most commonly, the first player would flick a marble along a few feet, then the next player would flick his marble and try to hit the first one. If he missed, the first player would go again. This would continue until one of the players hit one of his opponent's marbles. He would then win all the marbles that had been played. For some reason I was quite good at this game. I started off with just one marble that I borrowed from another boy and finished up with a sizeable collection.

Ciggies was a game where you could win a large collection of cigarette cards. There were two variations of this game, dropsies and flicksies. In dropsies the participants would stand up and the first boy would just drop his 'ciggie' (cigarette card) to the ground. The next to go would drop his and if it covered the first one he won them both. This was more difficult than it sounds since ciggies were usually very light and floated in the wind, so very rarely just fell straight.

The more popular game, though, was flicksies. In this, any number could join in and you had to hold your ciggie between your index and middle finger and flick it at the wall. Whoever had the ciggie that finished nearest the wall won all the others; this too was more difficult than it sounds as you had to be careful not to flick so hard that the ciggie hit the wall and bounced back a long way. There was a fine judgement in getting it just right. For both this and dropsies, the thicker the card the better and sometimes two cards were stuck together for that very reason. Some cards were even sold with gummed backs.

After a while, I wasn't too keen on this game since I didn't want to lose my cigarette cards as I found the information on the back of some of them very interesting. Two sets I can still remember well were a 'Kings and Queens' set, from which I learnt a lot about the history of British Kings and Queens, and 'Coach Companies', which featured such companies as Premier Blue, Empire's Best and Midland Red. There were also many sets of footballers and cricketers, which I collected. I used to buy my cigarette cards from a really tiny shop on the corner of Rushmore Road and Glyn Road, called The Cabin. As the name suggests, it was the size of a small shed and adults had to duck to get into it. The shop sold mixed packets of six cigarette cards costing 1d.

The other seasonal game, gobs, was played with five small cubes like dice, only without any numbers on the sides. There were two main variants of this game as well. The simplest consisted of tossing up one gob from the back of the hand and picking up one or more of the others from the ground while it was in the air and catching the tossed gob and so on until all five stones were picked up. The other was tossing up first one stone, then two, then three and so on from the palm of the hand, and catching them on the back of the hand. The winner was the first player to successfully complete whichever variant you were playing. There was no prize for this, just the satisfaction of winning.

As well as providing the space for somewhere to play, the playground also housed the toilets. There was one in the boys' playground and another in the girls' and they were the only toilets for pupils in the school. We didn't have the luxury of indoor toilets. If it rained or snowed, we were allowed to play in the hall or in our classrooms, but there was no such luck if you wanted to go to the toilet – you just had to brave the elements.

I mainly played all my games at playtime as I used to go home for lunch. This usually consisted of a sandwich of some sort and a glass of orange squash. Mum and I would have lunch at the kitchen table while listening to the radio. The programme we liked best was *Workers' Playtime*, which used to be broadcast live from a factory canteen 'somewhere in Britain'. This had begun as a wartime programme to help keep up morale at home but became so popular that it continued until well after the War. Usually, the bill consisted of a couple of singers and comedians. Some of the singers we first heard on these programmes included Julie Andrews, Anne Shelton, Dickie Valentine and the 'girl with the giggle in her voice', Alma Cogan. My favourites, though, were always the comedians and it was here that I first heard the likes of Ken Platt – 'I won't take me coat off – I'm not stoppin'', Al Read – 'You'll be lucky, I say you'll be lucky' and Tommy Trinder – 'You lucky people!' Oh yes, they all had their catchphrases. It was on this programme that we heard the following joke: 'A man came up to me the other day and said, "Have you seen a lorry load of monkeys pass this way?" So, I said to him, "Why, did you fall off it?"' I can't remember whose joke it was, and it might seem pretty innocuous, but Mum thought it was hilarious and repeated it for years afterwards.

Mum would always have lunch ready and waiting for me when I got in as she could be absolutely sure of the time. School broke up for lunch at 12.30; it took me seven minutes to walk home, so she was sure I'd be home by 12.37. However, one lunchtime, I wasn't home by 12.37; I wasn't even home by 1pm because this was the day they started work on converting the bomb site in Chatsworth Road to a block of flats. On my way back, I stopped to watch the lorries move onto the site, bringing in all the necessary machinery as well as the bulldozers ploughing up the rubble. It was a very exciting interruption to the normally routine day and I stood gazing in awe for ages until I suddenly remembered that I had to get home for lunch. When I eventually got back, Mum was very relieved to see me. I shudder to think what thoughts must have been going through her head about why I should be so late back, but she didn't say anything after I explained what had happened, though it did mean I missed most of *Workers' Playtime*.

By the time I was about nine years old, Mum said she wanted to get back to work. It wasn't really that we needed the money, just that she felt a bit lonely and isolated being on her own most of the day. She soon found a job near home at a toy factory in Brooksby's Walk. This meant that, for the first time, I had to have the dreaded school dinner. It was a ghastly experience. I was served up with a plate of horrible pulp, which I think was supposed to be minced meat of some description, but the 'meat' consisted mainly of inedible fat, skin and gristle accompanied by a single hard-boiled potato and some soggy, limp, mushy green vegetable that could have been cabbage, but might have been anything. Even the semolina dished up for afters was no better.

For someone used to home cooking, the food was simply appalling but there was more to come in this completely alien experience as, when I finished my dinner, I crossed my knife and fork on the plate. Bob Marriott, who was sitting next to me and an old hand at school dinners, was aghast. He said, 'You're not allowed to do that! You have to put them down beside each other.' This was the final straw. When my parents asked me what I thought of school dinners that night, I told them how terrible they were. So after just one day Mum gave up her job so that I wouldn't have to go through that torture any more. However, she was really feeling the strain of being at home, but she then had a brainwave when she saw that my school was advertising for dinner ladies. This was the answer, she thought: she could work and keep an eye on me at the same time. So, although the dinners didn't improve, consisting mainly of such delicacies as a slice of beef mince pie, a dollop of cottage pie or some glutinous mass masquerading as stew with a lump of mashed potato, scooped onto the plate with an ice-cream scoop, and cabbage followed by tapioca pudding (commonly known to us as 'frog spawn'), prunes and custard and sometimes just a plate of pink custard on its own, at least I had my mum there at dinnertimes.

Eventually, once I got used to the idea of staying at school for lunch, Mum went back to the toy factory. I have to say there was an added bonus in this for me as she used to bring home 'samples'. The toy she brought back the most often was a little cannon that fired matchsticks. I had several of these. Occasionally she also brought back a toy car. So, in the end, it was win-win all round. Mum felt a lot better as she was able to get out and enjoy the company of the other factory workers during the day and I got lots of new toys.

In my last year at Rushmore, I was made not only a milk monitor but a stair monitor as well. In those days, all schoolchildren were provided with a free 1/3 pint bottle of milk at morning break. As milk monitor, my job was to help get the crates ready in the hall for each class to take up to their room. My fellow monitors and I had to punch a hole in the top and push a straw through every bottle. This was all right most of the year, but in the depths of winter these bottles actually froze up and it was hard to push the straw through. My function as a stair monitor was to stand on the stairs at playtime, dinnertime and going-home time to make sure that no one ran. If they did, then we had to tell them to stop and if they still carried on running we had to report them to a teacher. It wasn't a job I enjoyed for it felt too much like being a snitch.

Towards the end of my school days at Rushmore, I had to take the dreaded 11-plus exam. If you passed then you went on to grammar school and if you failed it was the secondary modern. The 11-plus was created by the 1944 Butler Education Act and was supposed to establish a tripartite system of education, with an academic, a technical and a functional strand. Prevailing educational thinking at the time was that testing was an effective way of discovering to which strand a child was most suited. The results of the exam would be used to match a child's secondary school to their abilities and future career needs. However, when the system was implemented, hardly any technical schools actually appeared and the 11-plus came to be characterised merely as a competition for places at the prestigious grammar schools, so that, rather than allocating according to need or ability, it became seen as a question of passing or failing.

The examination itself consisted of three papers: arithmetic, writing and an IQ test. I passed the exam but that in itself led to two twists in my academic career. The first was that, in the school's own end-of-year test, I only came seventh in class. Every year the top eight in the A stream were awarded a prize, usually a book of some sort. That year Mr Moore decided that he would award prizes to the top six, plus two others whom he thought deserved a prize for their hard work even if they didn't finish high up in the exam. Dad was upset that this meant my not getting a prize. Personally, I wasn't really very bothered, but he went up to the school to see the Headmaster about this injustice.

The outcome of the meeting in some ways made the injustice seem even worse as it was a real case of 'Do you want the good news or the bad news?' The good news was that I had actually received the highest marks of anyone in the school for the 11-plus exam; the bad news was that I still wasn't getting a prize! Dad was absolutely incensed and he forbade me to go to Prize Giving Day, which was compulsory for all pupils to attend. He said it would upset me but I think it upset him more.

Although I didn't get a school prize, I was rewarded for having passed the 11-plus, firstly by my parents, who presented me with a signed Tom Graveney cricket bat (Graveney was my favourite cricketer). Secondly by Nan, Grandpa and Aunt Clara, who each bought me a Premium Bond. I still have them today, 56 years later at the time of writing, and they've never won me a sausage!

As far as upsetting news about the 11-plus and prizes went, that wasn't the end of the good news, bad news, as some time later the Headmaster asked to see Dad again and told him the good news, which was that my high 11-plus marks meant that, like John, I had been offered the chance of going to Christ's Hospital, Westminster or Bancroft's on a scholarship. The bad news was that he hadn't said anything until it was too late to apply as he felt I wasn't cut out to be away from home. Once again, Dad was furious. Although I suspect he didn't want me to go away either, he quite rightly reasoned it wasn't Mr Foreman's decision to make. There was also the point to take into consideration that, had I gone to Christ's Hospital, I wouldn't have been on my own as John would still be there in his last year and would be able to look after me.

Anyway, it never happened and I had to choose between three local grammar schools instead, Hackney Downs, Owen's and Parmiter's, all single-sex boys' schools. Hackney Downs was the nearest, and most of those who passed at Rushmore decided to go there, including my best friend, Andy. For some reason, I quite fancied Parmiter's. It had a better name locally and, although administered by the London County Council (L.C.C.) just like the other two, it had a certain degree of independence and still carried the status of 'public school'. I think Dad quite fancied this as well for it would go some way towards spiting Mr Foreman with the idea that I was going to a public school after all. So Parmiter's it was, along with Bob Marriott and Terry Gregory.

Before I left, I had one more run-in with Mr Brown. During the last week at school, it was traditional for those leaving to go round getting the teachers' autographs. All of them, except one, signed with no difficulty. That one was, of course, Mr Brown: he said you had to give him a reason why you wanted his autograph. We had been to a carol concert for schools at the Royal Festival Hall the previous Christmas and I'd noticed that he was a member of the London School Board organising committee for the event so my reason for getting him to sign was to say he was famous as he was on this committee and had his name printed in the programme. He said he wasn't famous and I should come back with a better reason. I told Dad about this and he suggested I just say to him that I wanted something to remember him by. On my way to school the following morning, I considered this and thought to myself that actually I didn't even like Mr Brown and didn't particularly want to remember him, so I just took the view, 'Sod it, if you can't sign my autograph book like all the other teachers, I really don't care!' And I never went back to him, hoping in time, without his autograph to remind me, he would simply fade from memory.

I still have my autograph book with all the teachers' signatures in it, including Mr Moore, Mr Wills, Mr Evans and Mr Bristow. There are many others, most of whose names I have long since forgotten. But, annoyingly, even though he is not there, one of the teachers I still remember the most, as can be seen from this chapter, is the one I hoped to forget.

CHAPTER THREE

RADIO FUN, *CASEY JONES* AND JACKETS FOR GOALPOSTS

When I wasn't scoring at cricket matches or attending drama classes, I used to play with my friends after school. Before we got down to this, however, there was the important matter of looking in on Reg's on the way home. Reg's was a newsagent situated at the corner of Millfields Road and Powerscroft Road and was my supplier of comics. Starting with *The Dandy*, my weekly purchases grew to include *The Beano*, *The Topper*, *The Beezer*, *Radio Fun* and, finally, *Junior Express*.

The Dandy was home to Korky the Cat, Keyhole Kate, Hungry Horace, Black Bob and, of course, the one and only Desperate Dan with his cow pies. *The Beano* included among its characters Biffo the Bear, the Bash Street Kids, Minnie the Minx and Dennis the Menace. Both magazines had been going since before the War but *The Topper* and *The Beezer* started during the 1950s so I was in at the start. Each one celebrated their inaugural edition by giving away a banger. This was a popular free gift at the time, which consisted of a triangular piece of card with paper partly stuck to the inside. The card was held at one corner and then with a sharp flick of the wrist the card would open out and the paper inside would make a mini sonic boom as it flipped out. As they were made of thin card and paper, they never lasted very long, but they were fun while you had them.

The Topper's front-page star was Mickey the Monkey, who was forever winning prizes in competitions, quite often a sandcastle competition, but not always. He would make the biggest, the brightest, the loudest and the best of whatever it was and he was always presented with his prize by the Mayor, who was naturally shown wearing his official chain. Most strips ended with the line, 'You win, Mickey.' This was repeated so often in the comic that it became a popular saying in our house, so that, whenever anyone won at cards or a board game, we would say, 'You win, Mickey.'

Radio Fun was a good source of ciggies as they often gave away free sets of cards depicting wireless personalities and sports stars. The comic itself featured strips based around leading radio personalities of the day such as Arthur Askey, Cardew 'the Cad' Robinson and Jewell and Warris. *Junior Express*'s most popular character was Wulf the Briton, who started life as a gladiator in Rome but later returned to Britain to lead the heroic struggle against the Roman invaders.

If the weather was fine, we would play outside. I was very fortunate living on a big field as we were able to play football or cricket, according to the season, very close to my home. Football meant throwing our jackets down to make the goalposts, the captains picking their teams and then play would commence. Although there were arguments, of course, about offside, the ball being too high, going for a throw-in and the rest of it, because we were all friends these never really got out of hand. If there were only three or four of us, we would play in front of the prefab and use the two trees to the side of the path as our goal and generally we played 'Three and in'. Someone was designated the goalie and the other two or three had to put the ball past him. When one boy managed to get three in, he would then go in goal. Sometimes we played 'tackling', other times 'passing'. If we played 'tackling', it was every boy for himself; if we played 'passing', then we were supposed to co-operate, although I think this game led to more arguments than any other. 'You should have passed, I could have scored', 'No, you couldn't, I had the best chance' and so on. Cricket followed much the same pattern, and if there were only three or four of us we played French cricket.

We also had running races round the field. Mum once knitted me a badge to sew on my shirt, bearing the title, 'Norman Harriers', with a picture of a Norman helmet. We could hold bicycle races too if enough boys with bikes turned up. One boy in particular earned himself one of Dad's nicknames because he always turned up on his bike. His real name was Robert Smith, but he came to be forever known in our family as 'Bike Robert'. He actually lived quite a long way from me, but loved cycling.

Picking to see who would be team captain or who would ride in the first race was a rigmarole in itself and we had several 'dipping games' to help us decide. The most popular was 'Dip, dip, dip, my little ship'. Everyone lined up and someone would go along the line, pointing at every boy in turn as each syllable was said. The full rhyme was 'Dip, dip, dip, my little ship, Sails on the water like a cup and saucer, You are not it!'. The boy who was not 'it' therefore dropped out and the whole thing was repeated. If there were a lot of us playing, this in itself could take some time! As we grew older, this rhyme sadly got corrupted as we discovered certain words that we could daringly use among ourselves that we couldn't use with our parents and teachers and so it got shortened to 'Dip, dip, dog shit, You are not it'.

Another dipping rhyme we had was 'Eenie meenie macaraca, Rare raa dominaca, Knikerbocka lollypoppa, Om pom push'. For some reason this was a favourite of Bob Marriott's, but hardly anyone else ever used it – I don't think we could remember the words. And then, of course, there was the now highly politically incorrect 'Eeny, meeny, minee, mo, Catch a nigger by the toe, If he hollers let him go, Eeny, meeny, minee, mo'. But, of course, it meant nothing to us in those days. Another variation was 'One potato'. Everyone in the line-up had to hold out his fist, pointing downwards, and the picker went along the line, hitting each fist in turn to the words 'One potato, two potato, three potato, four, Five potato, six potato, seven potato, more'. The fist that was hit on the word 'more' had to be lowered and then the whole process started again. This took twice as long, but at least you got a second chance in this one. These were also used for games of 'He' and 'Hide and Seek', both outside and in school.

When the weather wasn't so good, we didn't play outside and

normally I would just be left with my best friend, Andy. He and I both loved sport so if we couldn't do the real thing we'd play football, cricket and athletics with our toy soldiers, of which we had many. Many of these were still the old lead variety, but new plastic ones were just starting to come through. I say soldiers, but of course, although there were soldiers, probably the majority of them were cowboys and Indians. Every one of them was given a name relating to some characteristic or other of the soldier in question. Some I can still remember are Grey Indian, Black, Lay Down, Bugle, Silver Stripe, Sheriff, Mauve Shoot-both-ways, his brother, Yellow Shoot-both-ways, and one simply called Girl.

Our preferred game was cricket and the way this was played was to put two matchboxes on top of the dining-room table to represent the wickets. The fielding team would be spread out around the table, while the batsman would be held in front of one of the matchboxes and the bowler by the side of the other. The owner of the bowler would then hurl the ball – a piece of silver paper rolled up into a small ball – at the batsman while the owner of the batsman would take a swipe at the ball with his soldier. If he missed and the ball hit the matchbox he was out; if he hit it and it went straight to one of the fielders he was out caught, but if he hit it away from one of the fielders he could run. This was done by moving the batsman as quickly as possible to the other end and even back again if there was time for two runs, while the nearest fielder had to be pushed to the ball and then the ball could be thrown at the matchbox stumps in an attempt to run out the batsman. Grey Indian was probably the best batsman I owned because he was very big and heavy, so he covered the stumps up and could take a hefty swipe.

When we got fed up with that, we used to play board games. Monopoly, of course, but also Totopoly, Rich Uncle, Scoop, Careers and Buccaneer. My favourite of all these was Scoop, which did not involve throwing dice and moving round a board as the others did and which appealed to my love of reading. The object of the game was to fill the front page of a newspaper with stories and advertisements. Each player was given a blank newspaper front page to fill split into different size spaces. The stories and adverts were obtained by collecting cards from a central pile or by 'stealing' an opponent's card. To acquire a story, a player had to collect three Scoop cards – a reporter, a photographer and a telephone card. Once you had these, you had to use an ingenious cardboard telephone device to 'phone' your story through to the editor. By moving a small handle to the left and then returning it to its starting position, a message appeared randomly in the centre of the phone, saying either to print or 'spike' the story. If you could print it, the appropriate story card was taken from a pile and placed on the player's front page. One story I can remember was headlined 'TV Set That Will Pick Up The Past'. Players obtained advertisements by collecting a set of three Scoop cards – salesman, artist and advertiser's approval. Adverts included Lyle's Golden Syrup: 'spread a little happiness'; BOAC: 'fly worldwide in supreme jet comfort'; and Dinky Toys: 'with over 160 models and new additions every month'. The first to fill the front page was declared the winner.

When I was seven, I made my first visit to the local library in Brooksby's Walk, and this also became a regular after-school activity. I was a very keen reader and the first time I went there I found it a truly awe-inspiring sight to see so many books in one place. The first book I ever got out was Kenneth Grahame's *Wind in the Willows*. As I read it, I quickly became immersed in the life of the Riverbank with Ratty, Mole, Badger and, of course, the magnificent Toad of Toad Hall himself – 'Poop, poop'. Just like Mole, I was 'bewitched, entranced and fascinated'. I was right there with them as my imagination took me inside Ratty's little house and Toad's mansion. And I was with Toad in his car every inch of the way and on his side in the final battle, 'running round and round the room, and jumping over the chairs', whacking the ferrets, weasels and stoats with a big stick. I had never read a book like it and I couldn't wait to get back to the library to find more exciting volumes to read.

After *Wind in the Willows*, I discovered the 'Dr Dolittle' books by Hugh Lofting, Barbara Euphan Todd's *Worzel Gummidge*, *Biggles* by Captain W. E. Johns and, best of all, Anthony Buckeridge's 'Jennings' books. Although I loved playing with my friends and my family, the time spent reading books and immersed in my own world and my own imagination was very special to me so I always made sure I found time to do it.

After playing with my friends or visiting the library, I came home to have tea while I watched children's television. My favourite programmes were the many cowboy series then on, such as *Kit Carson*, *Hopalong Cassidy*, *Rin Tin Tin*, *Fury* and, best of all, *Range Rider*. Wednesdays was always a good day as it became a tradition to have steak and chips while watching *Casey Jones*, a Western with a bit of a difference as it was about a railroad engineer and his engine, the *Cannonball Express*. There were also some one-off Western mini-series, such as *The Cabin in the Clearing*. Other must-see television programmes were *Crackerjack*, *The Buccaneers*, George Cansdale's *Looking at Animals*, *Mr Pastry*, *Sooty*, *Twizzle*, *All Your Own* and my personal favourite, *Billy Bean and His Funny Machine* – 'Billy Bean built a machine to see what it would do. He built it out of sticks and stones and nuts and bolts and glue'.

In the early 1950s, television broadcasting hours were very restricted. There was little or no daytime broadcasting to speak of, and Children's Television at 5pm was the start of the television day. There was a short break, or interlude as they were then known, at 5.45, until the news came on at 6pm. During the interlude, the BBC showed some of their famous four-minute films, such as *The Potter's Wheel*, *The White Kitten* and my favourite, *London to Brighton in Four Minutes*. The news was only a very short bulletin and then there was another break until the evening programmes started at 7pm. During that break, I would either go back into the field to play with my friends, or amuse myself at home by playing with my soldiers or cars, or reading a book.

Dad used to come home from work at about 6.30pm and have his dinner, which normally consisted of larger portions of whatever Mum and I had already had. I mentioned having steak and chips on Wednesdays and that was really a bit of a mid-week treat. On other days, our dinner at that time would normally be something like spam fritters, smoked haddock, saveloys or faggots and pease pudding (the pease pudding having been made by Mum by boiling up split peas in a big

74

linen bag placed in the copper), sausage mash and onions (always referred to in the family simply as 'S.M.O.' except I never had the onions because I didn't like them), toad in the hole, fried mincemeat (which was mincemeat just dry-fried in the frying pan and served up with bubble and squeak) or egg and chips, the chips of course having been hand-cut and fried – no readymade frozen chips in those days. All very simple but absolutely delicious foods. Dinner was always followed by 'afters' – jelly and custard, apple or rhubarb pie and custard, tinned fruit (normally peaches or pineapple) and condensed milk, suet pudding with golden syrup or jam (also boiled up in the copper), rice pudding with the skin on top and blancmange, a particular favourite of mine. In the autumn, we often had blackberry pie made from blackberries Mum and I had picked ourselves in Epping Forest.

Sometimes, especially in the early part of the 1950s, Dad came home very late. This was because his journey had been badly affected by a good old-fashioned London 'pea-souper'. To many Londoners, these smogs had become something of a way of life but the worst smog struck not long after I started school in December 1952. For several days, the streets were filled with a smelly yellow fog that cut visibility down to just a few yards. The street lights were useless as all you could see was a dim glow. It was a very eerie atmosphere all round as sounds were muffled and people walked about with scarves over their mouths and noses in an attempt not to breathe in the foul air. Public transport was at a standstill as buses were unable to run. It was estimated that the effects of the smog killed upwards of 4,000 people.

The severity of the disruptions and adverse health effects forced the British Government to bring in various measures in an attempt to end the crisis, culminating in the Clean Air Act of 1956. Among other measures, the Act introduced smoke control areas in towns and cities in which only smokeless fuels could be burnt; it also included measures to relocate power stations away from populated areas and increased the height of some chimneys. It was hoped this would reduce the amount of smoke in the atmosphere and therefore the number and severity of smogs. Although it took some time to fully take effect, the Act was eventually successful in completely eliminating the London pea-souper. For the rest of the 1950s, however, smogs did continue to blight the capital and there were several occasions when Dad was forced to walk home from work, a distance of some three miles. At times, visibility was so bad that he got lost on the way home, even though he knew the route like the back of his hand. On those days, he arrived home very late indeed, but fortunately these were rare, and became even rarer as time passed.

By the time Dad had finished his dinner, television was back on and we usually watched the early evening programmes until it was bedtime. These included *The Grove Family* (Britain's first television soap), *Fabian of the Yard*, starring Bruce Seton, Eric Robinson's *Music for You* and the American comedy series *Amos 'n' Andy* and *Burns and Allen*. *Sportsview*, introduced by Peter Dimmock, was naturally very popular with Dad and me, though I'm not sure what Mum made of it. We also watched the very first cookery programmes to appear on television with TV's first chef, Philip Harben. Little could he have known what he started!

When ITV began in 1955, British viewing habits were revolutionised in two ways. Firstly, they filled the 6–7pm gap with programmes like *Emergency Ward 10*, ITV's first soap opera, and, secondly, they introduced advertising to television for the very first time, beginning with Gibbs SR toothpaste. Some of the early commercials were of truly epic proportions, especially those for petrol companies like Shell and Esso. They sometimes lasted anything up to three minutes and must have cost a fortune to produce and air. Our favourites were Omo with Mrs Bradshaw, who got her shirts so white you had to wear dark glasses to avoid the dazzle, and Murray Mints, the first company to inject some humour into their advertising with thirty-second cartoon commercials – 'Murray Mints, Murray Mints, the too good to hurry mints'. ITV also introduced popular quizzes to television, with Hughie Green's *Double Your Money* and Michael Miles' *Take Your Pick*, both transferred from Radio Luxembourg. Other popular ITV programmes included *Murder Bag*, which eventually transformed into *No Hiding Place*, starring Raymond Francis, *The Army Game* and American imports such as *I Love Lucy*, *I Married Joan* and *Dragnet* – 'The story you are about to see is true. Only the names have been changed to protect the innocent'.

In the early days, they also combined programmes with adverts by running what were called 'Admags'. The most popular of these was *Jim's Inn*, starring Jimmy and Maggie Hanley as the owners of a village pub. Each fifteen-minute episode consisted of customers coming into their pub to discuss the price and quality of a variety of real products over a pint. They were hugely popular at the time but the BBC objected to them on the grounds that they blurred the distinction between advertisements and proper programmes and amounted to sponsored programmes, at that time banned by ITV. They were eventually deemed misleading and unfair and were banned by an act of parliament in 1963.

The BBC fought back with programmes like *Hancock's Half Hour*, *This Is Your Life* with Eamonn Andrews and their own American imports such as *The Perry Como Show* and *Highway Patrol* with Broderick Crawford, which gave us two new catchphrases, 'Ten-Four' and 'Ten-Twenty', which were in constant use in our playground for a while.

By the time ITV arrived in 1955, a number of other houses in the street had television as well as us, but, just before the new channel started, we got a new set, a 17-inch Sobell, able to receive it so we were ready from day one. In the very early days, ITV was broadcast over the air waves on what was called Band Three, as opposed to BBC being broadcast on Band One. Bertha next door bought her new television a couple of months after the start of ITV but she was determined to let everyone know she was the proud owner of a set that could receive the new station. On the day it arrived, she got her husband to stay indoors monitoring it while she ran up and down the path outside with a piece of aerial wire in her hand attached to the television, shouting loudly, 'Can you see Band Three yet, Geoffrey?' Poor Geoffrey replied several times that he could, but this didn't stop Bertha running up and down, continuing to shout about Band Three! She only stopped when she was sure that the whole neighbourhood knew they were wealthy enough to afford a new television with ITV.

Although we watched a good deal of television, the wireless was still important and we carried on listening to a number of the popular programmes such as *Henry Hall's Guest Night* and *Have a Go* with Wilfred Pickles – 'Give him the money, Mabel'.

When I reached the age of ten and was allowed to stay up a bit later before bed, we started going to the pictures on a fairly regular basis. This began with *The Wizard of Oz*, and moved on to most of the big films of the 1950s, including war epics like *The Cruel Sea* and *The Colditz Story*, adventure films such as *The Buccaneer* and *The Story of Robin Hood and His Merrie Men*, Brian Rix comedies like *Dry Rot* and *Sailor Beware* and Dad's favourite, *The Story of Gilbert and Sullivan* starring Robert Morley and Maurice Evans.

We also went to the Hackney Empire to see live shows on a few occasions. By the mid-1950s, the old Victorian and Edwardian type of Music Hall show had mostly vanished but a few theatres still valiantly battled on, the Hackney Empire on Mare Street being one of them. I can remember seeing the comedian Terry Thomas, also one of the first drag acts, Mrs Shufflewick, and the Billy Cotton Bandshow there. To me live theatre was a wonderful experience and much more interesting and exciting than the cinema. The plush seating and surroundings made me feel as though we were going somewhere very special and I really looked forward to our all too rare visits to the Hackney Empire. These visits gave me a love of the theatre, which has lasted to this day.

CHAPTER FOUR

RATIONING, EEL PIES AND MUFFIN THE MULE

The weekend started at nine o'clock on Saturday morning when I got up to listen to Derek McCulloch, universally known as 'Uncle Mac', introduce *Children's Favourites* on the wireless with the familiar words 'Hello, children everywhere.' There then followed an hour of records requested by children of all ages, ranging from hymns and classical music to children's songs and novelty records. The most popular songs turned up regularly and it was always somewhat comforting to hear 'The Ugly Duckling', 'Tubby the Tuba', 'Three Billy Goats Gruff', 'The Happy Wanderer', 'The Laughing Policeman' and my personal favourite, 'The Runaway Train', week after week.

One week, I even sent in a request myself for 'Nymphs and Shepherds'. Written by Henry Purcell, this was one of the classical pieces that was played fairly regularly. Although I did quite like it, it wasn't my favourite and it was really Dad's influence that made me request it. He thought it would sound better if my name was read out asking for that rather than, say, 'Tubby the Tuba'. So I wrote in asking for it to be played for me and 'my brother also' as I felt I'd have more chance of getting my letter read out if I was requesting it for someone else as well as just me. The week after I'd requested it, Uncle Mac did indeed play the song, but, as he was reading out the names, Mum asked me what I wanted for breakfast so I missed it and I never knew if mine was one of the names read out or not. It was very frustrating; it might have been my first moment of national fame but I'll never know!

When the programme finished, we went out to the shops and stalls in Chatsworth Road. In the early fifties, some food was still rationed. Rationing had been introduced during the War to preserve food stocks, a vital necessity for an island nation. With the country still in bad shape following the end of the War, food rationing was only gradually faded out. Bread was the first to come off in 1948, while the last was meat and bacon, not taken off until June 1954. Families were issued with ration books, containing coupons for the various different commodities that had to be handed to the shopkeeper when buying goods. They removed the coupons while you handed over the appropriate amount of money. To buy most rationed items, each family had to register at one chosen shop for each type of foodstuff and the shopkeeper was then provided with enough food for registered customers only. As an example of this, we were registered for meat at a butcher's in Chatsworth Road called Gunner's and we had to buy all our meat there. There were two other butcher's shops in Chatsworth Road, Harry Blyth and Hammett's. I can remember my parents becoming increasingly disillusioned with Gunner's. They looked longingly into the windows of the other two butchers, who they felt offered better meat. In the end, after some prolonged correspondence with the Ministry of Food, Dad managed to get our designated butcher's shop changed to Blyth's. About a month later, meat rationing was ended.

For some reason, most of the shops and stalls we frequented were on the left-hand side going up from Millfields Road. The first, on the corner, was the Stadium Stores. This was a small shop piled almost up to the ceiling with cans and packets of groceries. There was only a narrow passage through to the one part of the counter that was free from clutter. This was where Mr Bogush, the owner, sat and where you bought your goods. The main thing we used this shop for was cat food. I was generally sent out to buy four tins of Kit-e-Kat. They were 7½d each, so four came to half a crown or 2/6d (12½p). For some reason, however, they came in packs of three, so Mr Bogush always had to break open one pack to give me the one to go with the other three. The Stadium Stores was also used for emergency supplies if we'd run out of something, but it was not on our general Saturday shopping route.

Next to the Stadium Stores was a café where we sometimes stopped to buy ice cream. They had a serving hatch that opened directly onto the street, and we would take a bowl along and they would scoop the ice cream straight into the bowl with wafers for Mum and Dad and a cornet for me. We never used the café itself and as far as I can remember we never actually stepped foot over its threshold. The only other shop we used in this lower part of Chatsworth Road was the greengrocer, Godlonton's. At that time everything was loose and you'd take your large shopping bag along, ask for 5lb of potatoes (or whatever) and they would just be tipped straight into your bag. We bought all our fruit and vegetables here including bananas, which Dad considered to be the height of luxury. Bananas had been very scarce during the War, which is what had led him to this conclusion and, even though they were not so difficult to find by the 1950s, he still treated them with the utmost respect. Because of this, we had them only very occasionally and, when we did, he always told us we weren't allowed to eat more than one a day.

Next door to Godlonton's was a shoe mender called Thomas. We would always re-sole or re-heel a shoe rather than throw it away and have to buy a new pair.

The shops we frequented on Saturdays were further up and included Gunner's, and later Blyth's and Hammett's after meat had come off ration, and Sorrell's, where we would buy our cooked meats, such as ham and liver sausage. A great favourite of Dad's, which we regularly bought here, was wurst, a German salami, which he fried with egg. I thought it was delicious.

Our chemist was formally known as Benjamin's, but we always called it Benjy's. There were a couple of chemist shops in Chatsworth Road, and the other was called Fox, Wells. They were both easily identifiable by the four brightly coloured carboys (large bottles) that stood in their window. Like the red and white striped pole that projected outside barber shops, these carboys were signs that immediately identified the type of shop it was.

Getting a prescription made up took a bit more work than it does these days when most items come as pre-packaged pills. Then, all the pills were loose in large jars and the chemist had to pour out the requisite number through a measuring device into a plain cardboard box. There also seemed to be a lot more medicine in bottles rather than tablets dispensed in those days – again poured out of a larger container into the chemist's own stock of bottles. Ointments and creams too were made up by the chemist, often grinding the ingredients in a pestle and mortar. It seemed a much harder job in those days than just picking the requisite boxes off a shelf.

As well as getting our prescriptions made up here, we used the chemist to get our film developed. This was in the days when photos were taken on 120 or 127 roll film, usually with just eight photos on the roll. After the photos were taken, the roll would be removed from the camera and taken to the chemist who would then send them away for developing. After about a week of eager anticipation, the photos and negatives would be returned in a small paper wallet and collected. All so different from today's instant digital age!

The baker we used was Carrington Brothers; here we bought Wonderloaf or Carrington's own baked split tin, which was wrapped in tissue paper. This was on the corner of Chatsworth Road and Rushmore Road.

On the opposite corner was an off-licence and next to that was Harry Shaw's magnificent corn shop. His whole shop, as well as the pavement in front, was full of sacks of seed and grain, such as barley and oats, which all together gave off a wonderful smell. We frequented the shop often to buy items such as lentils and butter beans and especially split peas, which Mum used to make pease pudding, a staple item of our diet, but you could find all types of food and pet food for sale in those sacks. You bought it by weight and the seeds or beans or whatever it was would be scooped up out of the sack and poured into a paper bag.

Next to the corn merchant was my favourite shop in Chatsworth Road, Willis's, the sweet shop. Most of its contents were just heaven! My absolute favourites were Refreshers but I also liked aniseed balls, bull's eyes, Love Hearts, blackjacks, rhubarb & custard and fruit salad (at a farthing each), sweet cigarettes, sherbet dabs, sherbet fountains and Spangles, which were small square boiled sweets in a packet and came in many different flavours, my favourite being the Old English packet containing liquorice, mint humbug, cough candy, butterscotch and pear drop flavours.

When I had a bit of extra cash, I was able to buy chocolate bars such as Fry's Five Boys, Tiffin, Punch and Milk Motoring. Another favourite was 'Spanish', which was what we always called liquorice and it came in various forms including long strings, wheels, pipe-shaped and even liquorice root. You could also buy packets of Smith's crisps here. There was only one flavour – plain. But they came with a little blue bag of salt that you had to undo and sprinkle over the crisps yourself, except that most times you couldn't because the salt had got damp and would just fall out of the bag in one lump. But we still loved the crisps whether they were all equally salted or not. Willis's was also where my parents would buy our Easter Eggs – it was such a thrill to see mine on Easter morning with curly white icing spelling out my name on the chocolate.

A little further along was Arthur Toms, noted eel and pie house. This was where we bought our pie and mash and eel liquor, the only takeaway we had in those days. Whenever we decided to have pie and mash, I would be sent off with a large basin and a jug to buy this ambrosia of the gods. The pies and mash would be put into the basin and the liquor poured into the jug. Pie 'n' mash and eel liquor was a longstanding cockney tradition dating back to at least the eighteenth century. Originally, the pie filling was eel caught in the River Thames but gradually meat took over as a filling and they were made from any meat that was cheap and available. By the twentieth century, the pie had become standardised to contain minced beef.

The pie itself is a normal pastry but it is important that, while it is firm and crusty on top, the bottom has to be soft. Originally, the accompanying liquor was made from the water used to cook the eels in, flavoured and coloured with parsley. Even after eels were no longer used as the filling, the liquor was still made with eel stock. Before starting on it, the pie had to be opened at the top and a liberal dose of vinegar poured in. The whole meal was then eaten with a spoon and fork, never a knife. In common with all other Pie & Mash shops, Toms continued the eel tradition by selling jellied eels as an additional accompaniment or a separate snack. These were eels chopped into rounds and boiled in water and vinegar and then allowed to cool. As eels are naturally gelatinous the cooking process released jelly, which solidified on cooling. This was bolstered by some aspic jelly made from eel bones and the whole dish was served up in a small bowl with vinegar and a liberal dose of pepper.

As an alternative to having cold jellied eels, you could have the eel stewed and eat it while still warm. In the front window of the shop was a large tray of live eels, wriggling away for all they were worth. If you wanted one with your pie and mash, you told Mr Toms which one you wanted and he'd hoick it out of the tray, cut its head off and drop it into a vat of steaming water. A few minutes later, it would be done to perfection, taken out of the vat and chopped into rounds to make a tasty supplement to your meal. Although we usually bought our pie and mash to take home, we did sometimes eat in the shop, and, here again, Arthur Toms followed the age-old tradition of white-tiled walls, a black-and-white patterned mosaic floor and marble-topped tables laid out in rows with bench seats on either side.

I still hold to the view that pie and mash is the best food in the world, even if nowadays you don't have to take your own jug and basin along to the shop.

There were two more grocer's shops on the left-hand side of the road, Tesco and Victor Value. When we first started using them, they were just like any other grocer's shop of the period, with the assistant fetching your shopping for you from the shelf or the stockroom. If you wanted a lot of shopping, it was normal to have it all written down and to hand the list to the assistant. However, quite early on, first Victor Value and then Tesco turned into self-service shops with baskets at the entrance so you could do the shopping yourself and take your purchases to the till. It was a completely novel idea but a sign of things to come. That there was an early Tesco 'supermarket' on Chatsworth Road was very appropriate as Jack Cohen, founder of the modern-day, multi-billion-pound worldwide business, began life as a market trader. His first stall was in Well Street in Hackney, his second in Hoxton and his third in this very same Chatsworth Road, some years before he started the famous Tesco brand name.

We probably used no more than three establishments regularly on the other side of the road. Right at the top, where Chatsworth Road changed its name to Brooksby's Walk, was the laundry where we used to take what we called our 'bagwash' once a week. No sitting in front of machines spinning your laundry round in those days. You took your washing in a large bag to the laundry and collected it a few days later, undried and unpressed and reeking of bleach.

Once, the laundry lost our bagwash and, in spite of Dad producing the receipt, they denied all responsibility for losing it. Dad was furious and wrote to our local M.P., Herbert Butler, who took up the case on our behalf. After several letters backwards and forwards, the laundry agreed to pay compensation, though they never accepted liability. It didn't really matter whether they did or not as Dad refused to use that laundry ever again.

Back in Chatsworth Road, the other two shops I loved were next to each other; the first was called the Biscuit Box, and it just sold biscuits. Like the corn merchant, the shop and the pavement outside were piled high with tins of loose biscuits. These were bought by weight, scooped out and placed in a paper bag. The tins of broken biscuits were our favourites, as you got a big variety of different biscuits for a lower price. Next door was Williams Brothers, a grocery store. They operated a loyalty token system. Every time you bought something, the cashier would give you tokens based on the amount spent and you could use these towards future purchases in the shop.

The only other shops we occasionally used on this side of the road were Macefield's, a dark and dingy stationer, and Bowman's, a clothes outfitters where I was taken every now and then to be fitted up for new shirts and short trousers.

The two shops in Chatsworth Road we fortunately never needed to go into were the two pawnbroker's shops with their three balls hanging up outside. To many, including my family and our neighbours, they were a reminder of the dark days of the 1930s Depression and most people lived in real fear of having to use their services. The windows were full of watches, rings and bracelets that must have once been someone's treasured possession. It was all very sad. We never bought anything from them, as my parents were acutely aware that those objects were only there through other people's misfortune.

On Saturday, the streets would be lined with all manner of market stalls. We bought smoked haddock from the fishmonger's stall, and Mum used to linger for ages at the haberdashery stall, where she would buy sewing materials and wool. The wool came in twisted skeins, so when she bought some I knew that would mean that some time later in the day I would be sat in an armchair with the skein draped round my outstretched arms while she unwound it to make it into a ball.

Mum spent most of her evenings knitting things for Dad or John or me, but very rarely for herself. She also darned all our socks. It's easy to forget in today's throwaway society that socks were hardly ever discarded. If a hole – known as a 'potato' – appeared in the heel, it was darned, and if a hole appeared in that it was darned again and again and again. It was very rare for a pair of socks to actually be thrown away. Dad always wore what he called 'army grey' socks.

One stall I particularly remember was the one belonging to the cat's meat man. This wasn't an open stall like all the others but a narrow enclosed trailer with a counter cut into the side. Here you could buy fresh meat for your cat, liver and such like, but our cat preferred Kit-e-Kat.

After returning from shopping on a Saturday morning, Dad and I would usually watch sport on television. They had some really interesting sport in those days which you never see onscreen now, such as hill climbing, when cars would try to get up a steep muddy hill and whoever got the furthest won. There was a driver and a passenger and the car would always start off okay, but would then reach a particularly muddy or steep part, at which point the driver and passenger would bounce up and down in the car trying to get some grip, but usually to no avail as it slid gracefully back down the hill. Motorcycle scrambling was another favourite of mine.

The unfaltering routine was that, at about three o'clock, Dad and I would go to visit his parents, known to me as Nanny and Grandpa Jacobs, while Mum usually visited her parents, Nanny and Grandpa Sinnott. I never ever went with Mum to visit them – it was always off to Chingford Hatch with Dad.

In fact, I never saw much of any of Mum's family. They hardly ever visited us and we rarely visited them either. She had five brothers and sisters but I only ever met three of them. Her father's side were from Co. Wexford in Ireland. My great-great-grandfather had been a blacksmith but my great-grandfather was a bit of a rogue and had spent a year in prison for getting married bigamously. On release, he went off with his 'second' wife and no one in the family ever saw or heard from him again. My grandfather was from his first marriage and he and his five brothers and two sisters lived with their mother in Hoxton in London. He was a naval man and had served in the Royal Navy during the First World War. After the War, he became a lockkeeper with the Port of London Authority. Nanny Sinnott was born in Pittsburgh, USA, in 1890, but her parents were both English and had only moved to America the year before her birth. Her male ancestors had been in the carpentry trade for at least two hundred years. When she was four, the family, which consisted of her parents, her three sisters and her twin brother, returned to Britain.

Very shortly after I was born, as part of the re-housing programme, which saw us get our prefab, Dad's parents, along with their two remaining 'at home' children, Uncle Bob and Aunt Clara, also moved out of their Bethnal Green flat. No prefab for them, they were housed in a new London County Council estate called the Friday Hill Estate in the leafy suburb of Chingford Hatch in Essex. Unbeknown to them I am sure, the building of the estate had been the subject of great controversy when first mooted. The good citizens of Chingford were not overjoyed at the prospect of a beauty spot being turned into a housing estate for East Enders, especially as many of them were 'not of British origin', which was a polite euphemism for being Jewish. However, in spite of the opposition, the estate was built and my grandparents now found themselves in a luxurious three-bedroom terraced house with a ground-floor passageway leading to a substantial back garden, making it semi-detached downstairs. The house was a far cry from the cramped conditions that they had known for all of their married lives, surrounded by flats and more flats in the heart of the East End. These houses even had an inside toilet and bathroom, an unheard-of luxury.

So, every Saturday afternoon, we would get the 35 bus at the stop on Lea Bridge Road and make the thirty-minute journey to visit my grandparents. We always took a small box of iced cakes as our contribution to the tea we would be getting when we arrived. In the early days, Grandpa, Uncle Bob and Aunt Clara were still working, and weren't always in when we arrived. Saturday was also visiting day for my uncle Albert and his wife, Aunt Evelyn, and eventually their children, my cousins Barbara and David, so I got to know them very well. But because Sunday was the day set aside for Uncles Joe and David to visit I never saw much of them. Dad had two more siblings who didn't have a regular visiting day, so I didn't see much of them either during this period. They were Aunt Julie, who lived with her husband, Isaac, and their four children in a prefab in Bethnal Green, and Uncle Bill, who was registered blind and was going through a lot of domestic difficulties at the time, eventually leading to a divorce from his wife, Sally. Following the divorce, he moved to a flat in Clapton, which meant that I did get to see more of him later on.

My memory of those afternoons and evenings in Chingford is that they always followed the same pattern. First, we would get a cup of tea on arrival and then a bit later, once Grandpa had arrived home, full tea would be served. The tea would consist of rollmop herrings, gefilte fish, bagels (pronounced 'bygles', please!) with cream cheese and smoked salmon. There was a big plate of watercress, bread and butter and, of course, our plate of cakes, all washed down with copious cups of tea. My favourite thing to do at those Saturday teas was to make myself a watercress sandwich.

Although not in the least bit religious, my grandparents were very proud of being Jewish and clung as much as they could to their roots, even though they were now probably the only Jewish family in the street. They still spoke some Yiddish and words like *Mazel Tov* (good luck), *nosh* (used both as a noun meaning a snack or as a verb meaning to eat), *schlep* (used as a noun to mean a long journey or as a verb meaning to carry something for some distance), *shtick* (used by us to mean laugh) and many others were in everyday use at my grandparents' house.

There was another discrepancy in their language compared to that used in our house, which was that they were not averse to using the odd swear word, something Mum and Dad never did. Never once did I hear them swear when I was growing up, but my nan in particular was forever calling someone an 'old bugger', while my aunt would join in with the view that someone was a 'cocky sod' or some such.

One thing that wasn't different about their language was that they spoke a lot of cockney rhyming slang but this was nothing new to me as Dad used it all the time. Words and phrases such as 'Almonds' [almond rocks] for socks, 'Sky Rocket' for pocket, 'Mincers' [mince pies] for eyes, 'Barnet' [Barnet Fair] for hair and many more were commonplace in both our houses.

As well as language, there were other big differences between their house and ours. The first was they had an upstairs, which was where their toilet was. In my young days, I was a bit scared of going upstairs as it was usually quite dark and my imagination conjured up ghosts that could jump out at me. I used to avoid going to the toilet as much as I could. There was one occasion when I really wanted to go but was trying to put it off. Dad noticed this and said to me, 'He's gone on holiday. I saw him packing his case earlier and going out the front door, so he won't be there tonight if you want to do a wee.'

The second difference was that my grandparents, aunt and uncle all smoked. Nan in particular was a chain-smoker; she was hardly ever without a Player's Weight or a Woodbine in her mouth. (In case you're wondering, she lived until she was eighty-nine!) My aunt favoured Bachelor's, while Grandpa and Uncle Bob preferred to roll their own. Neither of my parents smoked, so there was an unusually foggy atmosphere inside my grandparents' house.

The third difference, and one that continually amazed me, was that there was not a single book in their house. The only reading material they had was the *Daily Mirror*, with the 'Old Codgers' letters column. We had hundreds of books at home. As well as Dad's classical literature, my brother and I had lots of children's books of our own. I could never understand how my grandparents could possibly go through life without reading anything. Even at a very young age, this struck me as being quite strange.

One final difference between their house and ours was that they had a telephone. We never had one all the time we lived in the prefab, but Nan and Grandpa had one right from when they first moved to Chingford. Their phone number was Silverthorn 6290. If we wanted to use the phone when we were at home, we had to use one of the red telephone boxes that were then common around the streets of East London. Outside Rushmore Road School, there were two red boxes with a blue police box in the middle – not the TARDIS, but a real phone box used by the police.

One day after school, when I was about ten, I had to phone Dad at work to remind him to bring a piece of wood home with him as he had promised to make me a toy boat. As I went to use the phone, all my friends crowded round as it was unusual for a ten-year-old to do so and it made me feel a bit grown up. At that time you put your tuppence in the pay slot, dialled the number and when someone answered you had to press Button A, the money then dropped and the call was put through. If no one answered, you pressed Button B and got your money back. So, with all my friends looking on, I dialled the number and someone answered, so I pressed Button A. Unfortunately, it was the wrong number and a complete stranger answered so I lost my money and didn't have any more. My friends were not impressed by my first attempt at using a phone! Everything ended happily, however, when Dad brought the piece of wood home anyway.

After tea, we'd usually watch television. *Wyatt Earp* was a favourite, as was, in my younger days, *Whirligig*, introduced by Humphrey Lestocq and featuring Mr Turnip and Hank the cowboy, who was always having trouble with Mexican Pete, 'zee bold bandit'. Another favourite was *Billy Bunter of Greyfriars School*, with the splendid Gerald Campion: 'I say, you chaps,

Yaroooo!' Watching telly would usually be accompanied by a glass of Cydakin, a fizzy apple drink.

In summer, I might go out into the garden, especially after Barbara was old enough to play. Grandpa was a good gardener. There were flowers as well as some vegetable patches, including a runner bean trellis. They also kept a few chickens. Dad told me that before the War his grandfather had kept chickens in his backyard in Whitechapel, but could never bring himself to kill them so he had to call on his son, Woolf, my great-uncle, to perform the deed whenever they fancied some chicken soup. I don't know what Grandpa did as Uncle Woolf lived nowhere near Chingford, but I did notice a rapid turnover in chickens when I visited so I guess he wasn't quite so squeamish as his father.

If I stayed in, I'd usually spend some time talking to Grandpa, who was very keen on boxing and knew all about the history of the sport. We often discussed such weighty questions as 'Who was the greatest ever?' and so on. It gave me a big interest in the sport and, by the age of seven, I could name all the current world champions and a good many of the former champions too. Of course, it was a lot easier then as there was only one world controlling body and eight weights, so there were only eight champions to remember. At the time of writing, with the multiplicity of ruling bodies and plethora of weights, there are currently eighty-seven different world boxing champions!

Although they had no books, they did have a piano and sometimes we would sit round it, having a bit of a family singsong. Nan was the piano player – she couldn't read a note of music but could play anything you asked her to. The biggest favourites were the old Music Hall songs. Grandpa's favourite artistes were Eugene Stratton and Gus Elen, one of whose most famous songs was 'If It Wasn't for the 'Ouses In Between', which was very appropriate for our gatherings as one of the verses was:

Oh! It really is a wery pretty garden
And Chingford to the Eastward could be seen
Wiv a ladder and some glasses
You could see to 'Ackney Marshes
If it wasn't for the 'ouses in between.

But his favourite song was Billy Merson's 'The Spaniard That Blighted My Life', which he would deliver with great gusto.

Sometimes I would tinker around on the piano and was very pleased with myself one day when I managed, quite by chance, to knock out the first few notes of 'Three Coins in the Fountain' (in the right order, as Eric Morecambe might have said!), a very popular song of the day.

They also had a gramophone and sometimes played a few records, but in this medium they preferred Jewish songs. Particular favourites of theirs were Issy Bonn singing 'My Yiddishe Momme' and 'Did You Know The Negev?' The latter was particularly poignant and relevant to any family steeped in the Jewish tradition at this time. It began, 'Did you know the Negev when it was all sand? Then the desert Negev was the promised land...' and went on to explain how the Israelis had turned it into sustainable farmland and a homeland for the Jews. Of course, it had not been many years ago that the Jews had suffered appalling atrocities at the hands of Hitler and the

Nazi Party. Their pain had been deeply felt by all Jews, German and free, and when the state of Israel was set up after the War, they saw it as their homeland, even if they didn't live there. It was a time of hope for Jews everywhere.

I don't want to go into the rights or wrongs of the occupation or what has happened since as I know full well that, with complete justification, the Palestinians don't see the process the same way, but the feelings of the Jews at that time were that, after centuries of persecution and the recent horrors of the Nazi death camps, at last they had a safe haven, somewhere they could call home. Songs like 'Did You Know The Negev?' struck a deep chord with my grandparents; they played it proudly, as a symbol of their new hope.

Ironically, Uncle Albert, who took after his parents much more than Dad did in keeping the Jewish tradition alive, was a British soldier stationed in Palestine at the end of the War and his job involved trying to suppress the Jewish uprising and their attempts to found the nation state of Israel. It must have been a terrible dilemma for him as his sympathies would undoubtedly have been with the people he was forced to oppose.

The man who lived opposite my grandparents kept racing pigeons and, every evening after tea, he would let them out to fly loose around the houses. It was quite a spectacular site to see dozens of pigeons wheeling and circling around in the sky above the top of his house.

When Uncle Bob and Aunt Clara came home, they were nearly always presented with a bowl of lokshen soup as it was properly known, another standard Jewish delicacy. It was made by boiling up a chicken in a pot of water with carrots, parsnips and celery, a pinch of saffron and a large helping of lokshen, or vermicelli, as the manufacturer called it. Once ready, the chicken would be fished out, jointed and placed on a separate plate with roast potatoes. The soup would, naturally, be eaten with a spoon, while the chicken and potatoes would be picked up by hand. My aunt always used to give me the wing from her chicken as a little treat.

As an occasional change from lokshen soup, they would sometimes be given something Nan called 'vish splosh'. This was a soup made from any kind of meat and vegetables she could lay her hands on. I'm not sure if it was traditional or just something she concocted all by herself. Thinking back, they can't have been very strict Jews because they used to love a bit of bacon or pork in their vish splosh.

After they'd had their dinner, Uncle Bob would usually find time to play with me. I used to like him because he was very funny, just like an uncle should be! But he was also a bit of a rogue and soon became the black sheep of the family. He used to disappear for months at a time and no one knew where he went, then he would simply come home again as though nothing had happened and continue life with his mum and dad; he never said where he'd been. He ultimately fell out with Dad because, just before one of his disappearances, he borrowed our two-LP set of *The Pirates of Penzance*. Although Bob eventually returned as he always did, sadly our records did not. For Dad, there was nothing worse than having his beloved Gilbert and Sullivan records stolen so he never spoke to him again.

In 1955, Bob got married to Shirley Steer, who already had an illegitimate child called Dawn. She was promptly nicknamed 'Dripping', as there was a well-known brand of cooking margarine on the market called Dawn. It was hoped that now that Bob had married he would settle down, but just two years later he divorced Shirley and was off again. This time, he didn't turn up for over ten years. On his return, he married a Cypriot girl called Nicky, settled down to a very respectable life, had two children, Maroulla and John, and never went missing again. It wasn't until many years later that we discovered that just before his ten-year disappearance he'd had a daughter with Shirley, called Wendy.

Three years after Uncle Bob left, Shirley remarried and emigrated to Australia with her daughters and new husband. No one heard anything from them until Wendy contacted me via a Family History website in 2010, trying to find out about her father. He left when she was still a small baby, so she never knew him. She had asked her mother about him when she was growing up, but Bob's betrayal still hurt and Shirley refused to talk about him. I was flabbergasted when she contacted me as I had absolutely no idea of her existence.

Finally, before getting the bus back home, we might play a few games or watch a bit of telly. The games we played were either card games, shove ha'penny or 'fives and threes', a dominoes-based game. The card games were usually cribbage or klabberjass, known to us as 'clobby', a game popular among Jewish communities. It was quite an obsession in our family – everyone seemed to be an expert clobby player. I too became very good at it, but sadly none of my friends had ever heard of the game, let alone played it, so I could only practise my skills with the family.

If we watched television, it was usually to see *In Town Tonight*, *The Billy Cotton Band Show*, with the familiar catchphrase 'Wakey! Wakey!' or *Dixon of Dock Green* – 'Evenin' all'. I can also remember a couple of serials, one called *The Teckman Biography*, a Francis Durbridge mystery starring Patrick Barr (or 'television with knobs on' as Dad called him because of his frequent appearances in television drama) and the other one, *The Trollenberg Terror*, a science fiction story with some scary monsters, or at least they were to me at the age of eight or nine. After one episode, which I must have thought particularly good, I said to Dad that I had to tell my friends at school about this. 'Don't you dare!' he warned. 'I don't want your teachers finding out that I let you stay up late to watch these sorts of films on television.'

After taking the half-hour bus journey home, we'd arrive back about the same time as Mum did. Until I was much older, I never met my other grandfather. Nanny Sinnott used to come and visit us quite often during the week, so I saw a fair bit of her. I can remember one occasion when Mum went out shopping and Nan minded me. She made me a cup of hot Bovril. I took one sip and thought, 'This is terrible,' but I didn't like to say anything to her. So I just sat with this cup of Bovril, hoping and praying Mum would come home soon so I could tell her I didn't want it.

I found out when I was thirteen that the reason I never visited my grandfather was that in their younger days he had been violent and physically abusive to Nan so Dad would have nothing to do with him. Mum told me that he came home drunk on many occasions and tipped the table up with all their dinners on it. On one particular occasion, he kicked Nan so hard that she crashed into the table and was knocked unconscious. Mum and her sister, my aunt Nell, carried her upstairs and put her to bed. Mum then came down to the kitchen and started searching through the cutlery drawer for a knife. Suddenly, Grandpa appeared in the doorway. 'What are you doing?' he demanded. 'I'm going to kill you,' she replied. He slammed the box shut, scooped her up under his arm and manhandled her to bed, where she spent the rest of the night sobbing.

One day, after he'd knocked Nan about for simply asking for housekeeping money, she went to Tower Bridge police station to report him. The policeman said there was nothing he could do about it because the police weren't allowed to interfere in domestic quarrels. Nan replied, 'All right, if there's a murder tonight it will be your fault.'

Another time when he came home and started on Nan, Mum's brother, my uncle Bill, tried to stop him hitting her and they ended up fighting. Grandpa threw him out of the house bodily and told him he was never to come back: he was only eleven. He then slammed the door behind him and physically stopped Nan going after him. It wasn't until he eventually fell asleep several hours later that she was able to get out and look for Bill. By that time, she was frantic with worry as she had no idea where he could have gone to, so she just set off walking round the local streets, shouting out his name. Finally, she found him sitting in a shop doorway, crying his heart out. She picked him up and held him tightly for a moment or two while she too had a good cry. Nan knew she couldn't take him home as she was afraid what her husband might do to him, so she took him to a friend's house and, after explaining what had happened, asked if Bill could stay there for a couple of nights till it was safe to come home. On hearing what had happened, her friend agreed to take him in for a short while and to look after him. In the end, Bill stayed with her until he got married, ten years later.

After listening to these stories, I completely understood why my parents wanted nothing to do with my grandfather and why they didn't want me to see him. What a complete bastard! Mum told me that some time after she'd left home to get married she asked Nan why she put up with him and didn't leave him. Her sad reply was: 'Where would I go with six children and no money?' She must have felt so lonely and so trapped.

The only time the Saturday routine ever varied was when we went down to Sussex to see my brother John, which happened about once or twice each term. We got the 38 bus to Victoria station, where we boarded the train to Horsham before changing onto a small country line still operated by a steam locomotive. As we puffed our way through the open countryside, it was like being transported into a different world. All you could see around were green meadows and cows grazing in the fields. Although we lived on a field in London ourselves, it was nothing like this. There was no traffic, no shops, not even any houses to spoil the view, just acres and acres of the green rolling South Downs. When we arrived at Christ's Hospital's own specially built halt, we took the long walk up the path to the school gates, where John would be waiting for us. Most times we just used to get back on the train and go into Horsham for lunch at The Carfax, but sometimes, especially in the summer term, he would take us to local places of interest, such as Arundel Castle, Box Hill or Bognor Regis. Sadly, the day was up all too quickly and we had to make our way back to the station for the return journey, usually with a small present Mum and Dad had bought me in Horsham for 'being good'. This was normally a small book of dot-to-dot puzzles or a magic painting book, where you brushed each page just with water and a coloured picture would magically appear.

Sometimes the train took us back to London Bridge rather than Victoria. I didn't like this, as we had to stand and wait for our bus at the stop outside Southwark Cathedral, and for some reason I found this really scary. To me the great big building looming up out of the dark seemed to hide all sorts of terrors, especially as I could see the graveyard at the side.

After all the excitement of a typical Saturday with its shopping expeditions and family visits, Sunday was much more relaxed. In those days, practically no shops were open on a Sunday; in fact, hardly anything was open and very few people worked. Sunday was a family day.

Our Sunday always began with me getting into Dad's bed and us reading the sports pages together while Mum went to make breakfast. Our Sunday newspapers were *The People* and *Reynold's News*, both radical Labour Party-leaning papers, as was our daily paper, the *Daily Herald*. Dad had been a Labour Party supporter all his life, as were all his family and, indeed, it seemed, everybody else in the East End of London. Politics were much more divided on class lines in those days and it would have been very hard to find a working-class Conservative voter. In fact, from 1945 until 1965, the year I moved away and the old Metropolitan Borough of Hackney was merged with Shoreditch and Stoke Newington to form the new London Borough of Hackney, the only non-Labour councillors on the Council were from the Communist Party. Not a Tory in sight! The Liberal Party barely existed apart from on the Celtic fringes in Scotland, Wales and Devon and Cornwall, and the country was much more polarised between Labour and Conservative.

Of course, none of this mattered to me, reading the sports pages with Dad and waiting for breakfast. Mum usually made a boiled egg with 'soldiers' (thin, finger-like strips of toast), or bread and dripping, served with plenty of salt and pepper. My word, it was delicious! No worries about cholesterol levels in those days. Occasionally, we would have eggs and bacon as a treat.

Once we were up, Dad might do a few jobs around the house. One I always found fascinating was the cleaning of the gutters. Living on a field surrounded by trees meant that they frequently filled up with soggy leaves, so he had to get the stepladder up and clear them all out. It was an absolutely filthy job and he got covered in mud and slime. Meanwhile, I would usually be playing with my toys. I had a large collection of lead soldiers, cowboys, Indians and the like – so big, in fact, it's a wonder I didn't suffer from lead poisoning! I would set them up on the table with a toy fort I had and one lot of soldiers had to defend the fort from the rest. Under the table was where I would race my little tin cars and buses.

By the time I was about seven or eight, Dad and I would often take a walk down Millfields Road and cross the little iron bridge to Hackney Marshes to see a football match. Hackney Marshes was, and still is, home to the largest number of football pitches on a single area of open space anywhere in the world. In the 1950s, there were something like a hundred pitches, all crammed tight on one another so there was little room to stand on the touchline to watch. Several local leagues played their matches there; we supported the Hackney and Leyton League and used to go and search out that league's matches, not an easy thing to do with that number of pitches. Our favourite teams were United Services, who played in orange and black, Pembury (white with a red 'V') and Grove United (claret and blue). We got to know some of the better players and some of the touchline supporters, most of whom thought they could do a much better job than the manager or players! One in particular seemed to have it in for a player called Cotterell. He was a short, stocky player who played on the left wing for Grove United. For some reason he had gathered his own anti-fan club of one. Several times we saw the same oldish, balding man turn up at Grove United games just so he could abuse poor old Cotterell. He would run up and down Grove's left touchline, shouting, 'Pass it, you idiot!', 'What was that supposed to be?', 'You're useless!' and so on. At half-time he would swap sides so he could continue abusing the poor bloke. We always thought Cotterell was quite a decent player but he had obviously done something to upset this man. How he managed to put up with it, week after week, I don't know. Perhaps it was his father?

The top game in the league each week was played at Leyton F.C.'s football ground behind the Hare and Hounds pub in Lea Bridge Road, a bus ride away from our house. This was a proper football ground with a small stand. If it was a match we particularly wanted to see, we were prepared to fork out the small admission charge even though the matches on the Marshes were free. One of the regular spectacles at the Hare and Hounds was the sight of Alfie Stokes, a prominent Tottenham Hotspur player of the time, in the crowd, running a book on the result. There was a continuous stream of people going up to him throughout the game, asking, 'What's the odds, Alfie?'

On summer Sundays, we sometimes used to get the bus to Epping Forest. At that time, some services were extended to run to the forest, so the 35, which normally only went as far as Chingford Hatch, was extended to High Beech, in the heart of the forest. And we would also catch the 38A to the exotic-sounding Loughton and have a look round. We might also go 'down the Lane'. This was Petticoat Lane, the famous market street in Whitechapel. For Dad, this was like a return home as he and his family had originally come from the Aldgate/Whitechapel area and could date their ancestry in the area back to the 1660s.

One particular ancestral line, the Belascos, must have been among the very first Jews to be allowed into this country under Oliver Cromwell (Jews had been expelled from England by Edward I in 1290 and were not allowed back until the 1650s). Records show that my eight-times great-grandfather, Miyara Belasco, was born in London c.1670, the son of Portuguese-Jewish immigrants. He may have been a night watchman at the Jewish cemetery in London, certainly a number of his descendants were.

In the early nineteenth century, Aby Belasco became a famous boxer, who was once described as 'a boxer of superior talent, a master of the science, not wanting for game, not deficient in strength, of an athletic make, a penetrating eye, and in the ring full of life and activity'. After he retired, he became a licensed victualler in Whitechapel but sadly he lost all the money he had made boxing and descended into being 'a keeper of low gambling houses, night houses, supper rooms, and such like resorts of midnight and morning debauchery, which brought him into repeated conflicts with the law', as he was once described. His brother, Samuel, was transported to Australia for seven years for picking pockets but generally my ancestors were more law-abiding, if poor, and throughout the eighteenth and nineteenth centuries were mostly market traders selling general goods, second-hand clothes and fruit, most probably in the very same Petticoat Lane Market we were now visiting. The first actual Jacobs ancestor arrived here in the late eighteenth century as an immigrant from Germany. All my Jewish ancestral lines show early settlement in this country and were well settled here long before the main influx of Jews from Eastern Europe in the late nineteenth/early twentieth centuries. In fact, Nan didn't have a lot of time for the 'newcomers' and often referred to them as 'Polacks', whichever country they actually came from.

On Sunday mornings, this market was the vibrant hub of the East End, with thousands of visitors from all over the world jostling for a good look at the wares on offer. Dad used to look for bargains of any sort – he wasn't fussy what it was so long as it was good value. We'd also look in on the nearby Brick Lane Flower Market and the animal market in Club Row. You would always hear the animal market long before you could actually see anything, as there would be a cacophony of howling dogs, together with a chorus of bird song. At the market itself, there would be dogs of every breed, size, colour and temperament, along with row upon row of cages, containing exotic birds from all around the world. It was like being transported to a foreign country and I would imagine myself in the African jungle or on a boat travelling up the Amazon, listening to all these beautiful songbirds.

In spite of the excitement engendered by all of this, my favourite stop was at Woolf Rees's drinks stall. Here you would find a wide variety of different types of juice and squashes. For someone mainly used to orange squash, it was stunning to see such a plethora of different colours and flavours. My favourite was what I called the 'red drink', which was actually raspberry juice. Boy, it tasted good!

Occasionally, on our visits to Petticoat Lane we would see the famous racing-tipster known as Ras Prince Monolulu. He was a well-known flamboyant figure, who carried a huge shooting stick-cum-umbrella and wore an ostentatious ostrich feather headdress, a multi-coloured cloak and gaiters and a huge scarf wrapped around his waist. As he strode along the street he would exclaim, 'I gotta horse, I gotta horse', which meant that he would let you have the name of a 'sure-fire' winner in an upcoming horse race for a small consideration.

Although he styled himself 'Ras Prince', he was in fact born Peter Carl McKay in 1881 and was originally from the US Virgin Islands. He arrived in Britain in 1902 and, after a year of mostly menial work, managed to join the chorus of the first all-black West End musical show, *In Dahomey*. When it came to the end of its run, he went to Europe as an entertainer in a travelling roadshow. After the First World War, he began work for an Irish tipster but quickly went solo and took to shouting, 'I gotta horse' after seeing the religious revivalist Gypsy Daniels shouting, 'I've got heaven' to attract his crowds. In 1920, he reputedly won £8,000 on the Derby when he put all his money on an unfancied horse called Spion Kop and his reputation as a tipster was sealed.

One morning, he strode right up to Dad and me and stopped in front of us. He looked at me and said, 'I gotta horse... but I also gotta penny and you can have it.' And he gave me a shiny new penny. That must have been the first time I ever met anyone famous and I got a penny for it too.

On our return from football, Epping Forest or the Lane, Dad would put the gramophone on – nearly always Gilbert and Sullivan, of course. The only LPs we had were Gilbert and Sullivan operas. Generally, our records were the commonly available 78 r.p.m. These could be 7", 10" or 12", playing from about two to five minutes per side. Such records were usually sold separately, in brown paper or cardboard sleeves that were sometimes plain and sometimes printed to show the producer or the retailer's name. Generally, the sleeves had a circular cutout, allowing the record label to be seen. Again most of these were Gilbert and Sullivan recordings. We did have a number of other classical recordings as well, though no popular music; also a couple of curious records, which were HMV sampler records and contained several tracks, each playing about thirty seconds or even less of a particular song.

At the end of each track, there was a spoken announcement that the full version was available on such and such HMV catalogue number. We had one devoted entirely to G&S and another to other songs. The only one I can remember on this was Noël Coward's 'Mad Dogs and Englishmen'. I also had a couple of children's records. One was the Henry Hall Orchestra playing 'The Teddy Bears' Picnic' with 'Here Comes the Bogeyman' on the reverse and the other was Mel Blanc singing the Bugs Bunny song 'I'm Glad to Be the Way I Am', with Sylvester and Tweety Pie on the reverse, singing, 'I Taut I Taw a Puddy Tat'.

The 78s were made of shellac (a naturally found plastic made from insect resin, which was used in the production of gramophone records from the late nineteenth century until vinyl began to replace it in the late 1950s), which made them very fragile, and many were the records that broke and had to be thrown away. The other problem with these old records was the number of needles you'd get through. It was recommended that one needle only be used for one or two plays and then discarded. Using it a third time could damage the grooves on the record, but we often chanced it on the grounds of saving money. Needles came in boxes of 50 or 100.

While listening to the music, Dad would be getting Sunday lunch ready. It was always Dad who did that job and not Mum. Like my aunt and uncle when they came in from work, we too quite often had lokshen soup. Bought chickens at that time weren't like the prepackaged, prepared chickens you buy today, and the first thing Dad had to do was pluck all the feathers and singe the chicken with a lighted piece of paper to get off the 'stubble'. He would then open it up and take out the giblets and, quite often, some eggs. These came in varying sizes, from tiny up to full-size with a shell on, although this was something of a rarity. The giblets and those eggs big enough to eat were thrown into the cooking pot with the chicken. This was boiled up and served as in my grandparents' house. I was always given all the eggs and usually the liver, while the other giblets were shared out between Mum and Dad, Dad always having the neck.

About one Sunday a month, we had a roast dinner. Pork, lamb and beef all took their turn, along with roast potatoes and, usually, cabbage. Occasionally we had salt beef but this needed a bit of planning and preparation as Mum had to go to the butcher's to pick out a piece of beef the week or even two weeks before we had it. The butcher then pickled the beef in brine for at least a week – ten days was better – and we would pick it up on the Saturday, ready to have on Sunday. This was always served with pease pudding, cabbage and carrots. When we had a roast or salt beef, I was sent across to Pete's off-licence to get a bottle of fizzy drink.

Sunday lunch was always accompanied by the radio. Our favourite programmes were the sit-coms of the day and included *Educating Archie* starring Peter Brough, the world's worst ventriloquist, and his dummy, Archie Andrews. When we saw him on television, we realised just why he appeared mainly on the radio! This show introduced a number of young comedians to a wider audience, including Tony Hancock, Benny Hill, Dick Emery and Max Bygraves, who created two long-lasting catchphrases, 'I've arrived and to prove it I'm here!' and 'A good idea, son!' Other Sunday lunchtime listening in the fifties included *Life with the Lyons*, starring Ben Lyon, Bebe Daniels and their children, Richard and Barbara, *Take it From Here* with Jimmy Edwards, Dick Bentley and June Whitfield, and *A Life of Bliss* featuring George Cole, Nora Swinburne and Esmond Knight, with Percy Edwards as Psyche the dog. The other must-listen-to programme was *Two-Way Family Favourites*, a record request programme for those serving in the armed forces abroad, mainly in Germany, and their families at home.

After dinner, we would usually settle down to some family games. As I got older, these became more complicated. When I was five or six, this would mostly be snap or old maid, or some such, but, as I grew older, the card games became more taxing, rising up through knock-out whist and rummy to cribbage and, of course, clobby. Being a woodcarver, Dad had produced a beautifully carved cribbage board, which we used for scoring.

Sometimes, though it was quite rare, we would go and visit another member of the family on Sunday afternoon. On one occasion when I was about six, I was told we were going to visit my aunt Sally (Mum's sister). This disruption to my routine was not met with enthusiasm. 'Do we have to go?' I complained. Dad's reply was: 'Put your coat on.' So, reluctantly and dragging my feet as much as I could, I accompanied my parents to the bus stop, where we got the bus to Bethnal Green Underground station and caught the Tube. But when we got to Aunt Sally's I discovered that I had a cousin, John, who was about a year younger than me and had the biggest collection of toys of anyone I knew. When the time came to go home, I was playing with his fire engine and I said, 'Do we have to go?' Dad's reply, somewhat predictably, was: 'Put your coat on.'

Our most frequent visits were to Uncle Albert, Dad's

brother. He lived in an old Victorian two-bedroom terraced house in Jane Street, Stepney. The house was a real throwback to the bad old days as it had no bathroom and no inside toilet and a very small scullery masquerading as a kitchen. It was very cramped; a situation made worse by the fact that Aunt Evelyn's mother was living with them. Always referred to as 'Mrs Margetts' by my uncle and my cousin Barbara, she had one tooth in the middle of her mouth and that was it. I never saw her wear dentures. One time when we had tea there, we saw her put a pickled onion in her mouth and try to lance it with her one tooth. She missed and the onion shot out onto the table. But she was nothing if not a trier and this attempt to spear the pickled onion was repeated several times before she finally managed it. I could see my parents finding it very difficult to keep a straight face.

Only once can I remember us visiting someone who wasn't a relative and this was when Dad took us to meet one of his old army friends, Harry Hudson. Harry lived in an old Victorian terraced house, much like Uncle Albert's. He had a teenage son, also called Harry, so he was referred to as 'Harry Half', or, in their cockney accent, ''Arry 'arf', to distinguish him from the head of the household. Their house had a very narrow passageway leading from the scullery to the living room, wide enough for just one person at a time, so any time anyone left the scullery to go to the living room, or vice versa, they would shout that they were on their way to prevent anyone else from making the journey in the opposite direction. Quite often during that afternoon visit we heard the cry, ''Arry 'Arf comin' frough!'

But normally we stayed at home on Sunday afternoons. Sunday teatime was usually a bit of a fishy affair, with either sardines on toast or a mixture of shellfish we had bought from an itinerant street vendor who used to come down our street most Sundays, selling winkles, shrimps, cockles, mussels and whelks. We'd sometimes buy a selection of these delicacies and have them with bread and butter. Personally, I could never get to grips with winkles as they were too fiddly, having to extricate the little bit of meat there was from a shell with a safety pin. John amused the family by making winkle sandwiches. He'd spend what seemed like hours taking the winkles out and then lining them up on a piece of bread. I can't remember how many made up one sandwich but it was a fair few!

We had a number of other street traders in those days who would drive round the streets, selling their wares or offering their services. The other common trader was the ice cream man, who came round on a tricycle with a large freezer on the front. His range was a bit restricted as he only carried vanilla and strawberry ice-cream bricks as well as wafers and cornets, plus a few choc ices – no lollies.

There was the knife grinder who would call, asking if we had any knives or blades that needed sharpening. I believe he also provided a service in banging out dents in saucepans but we never called on his expertise in this field. The other fairly common trader was the rag and bone man, who used to cry out something that sounded like 'Anyolraganombrey?'. It wasn't until years later that I realised what he must have been trying to say was: 'Any old rags and bones?' He was one of the last people I ever saw using a horse and cart for his means of transport.

A stout, shortish man, he sat perched high up on a bench at the front of the cart, holding the reins of his horse. He always looked very scruffy, as if wearing the cast-off clothes that people gave him – and perhaps he was. Usually, he stopped in the middle of the street waiting for people to come out to him – no problem with holding up the traffic because mostly there wasn't any. In the days before charity shops, it was a good way of getting rid of old clothes and many's the time Mum, along with a number of the neighbours, would bundle some up and take them out to him. He would give her a few pennies for her trouble. We never gave him any bones, though.

Occasionally, a fishmonger came round the streets in a small van; he had a reasonable range of fish, but we preferred the fish stall in the market as it always seemed to be better prepared and there was a wider selection. Like everyone else, we had our milk delivered every day by the Co-op milkman in his hand-pulled float. He used to knock once a week and, because it was the Co-op, we had to give him our number so we could get our 'divi' paid. I heard that number so often I can still remember it to this day – 522782. 'Divi', as it was universally known, was short for dividend and as long as you joined the Co-op by filling in the membership form you were entitled to a share of the profits because the Co-op was (and still is) owned by its members. Every time you made a purchase, whether it was milk from the milkman or in a Co-op shop, the amount you spent was entered into a small passbook and twice a year you had to take your book along to a Co-op shop – our nearest was in Mare Street – and you would get a rebate based on how much you'd spent.

At one time, we had bread delivered by a baker's van, but this was a short-lived phenomenon as he used to turn up quite late and Mum wanted the bread delivered early. The funny thing was that he used to deliver in a small four-wheeled van. The week after we stopped using him, we noticed he'd been reduced to a three-wheeled van.

During our Sunday tea, we usually watched children's television as the times coincided nicely. In my younger days, I saw *Muffin the Mule* with Annette Mills, my favourite programme. As I got older and ITV began in 1955, I began watching Vincent Ball introduce programmes such as *The Adventures of Robin Hood* starring Richard Greene and *Roy Rogers*. After tea and television, there was a bit more time for play, usually while *Down Your Way* was on the wireless, and then it was into the bath, ready for bed. After my bath, I listened to *Dick Barton Special Agent*, which had an especially exciting theme tune called 'Devil's Gallop' and, in later days, *Journey Into Space* with Jet Morgan, Doc, Mitch and Lemmy. When I got older and bedtime became later, I'd watch a bit more television. *What's My Line?* with the grumpy Gilbert Harding, David Nixon, Lady Isobel Barnett and Barbara Kelly and hosted by Eamonn Andrews and *Sunday Night at the London Palladium* became favourites of ours.

Then it was off to bed. And so ended the weekend and I was all ready for school again the next day.

CHAPTER FIVE

HAMPSTEAD HEATH, DODGEMS AND THE FOUR-MINUTE MILE

Easter saw the first visit of the fair. Just across Lea Bridge Road, next to North Millfields, was a fairground used three times a year: Easter, Whitsun and August Bank Holiday. For a few days before it was due to open, we'd see the showmen turning up in their gaudily decorated caravans and lorries bringing their own particular ride or sideshow along. It always seemed to me that these people led the most romantic way of life, going from place to place, travelling the country, setting up fairgrounds. What a life they must have led!

It was a very exciting time and the Easter Fair was one of the highlights of my year. The official opening date was Good Friday, but we always used to go over on Thursday evening on the pretext of seeing if they were ready yet. They always were and, gee whizz, what a sight met our eyes! The coloured

119

lights, the smells of hot dogs, doughnuts, candy floss and petrol generators, the barkers (especially 'Ol' Billy Fairplay all the way from Holloway') bawling their attractions out to the crowd and the screams of people on the rides created an atmosphere that took me completely away from my everyday world. For the hour or so we stayed, it was like being in Paradise. There were the rides such as the dodgems, the waltzer, the Brooklands speedway racing track and, the centrepiece of the fair, the large gaily painted carousel with its golden galloping horses and the organ playing in the background; there were the game stalls, the coconut shy, roll the pennies, hoop-la and fishing for ducks; and sideshows like the boxing booth, where the 'Champion' challenged all-comers, the fortune teller and even freak shows with 'The Bearded Lady', 'The World's Smallest Man' and 'The Rubber Man'. Dad used to take me on the dodgems and we would also have a go at some of the games, quite often winning a goldfish or a cheap china fairing. Candy floss was a must and sometimes, if Dad was in a particularly good mood, a doughnut as well.

The fair stayed for about a week and then they all moved off to their next location. We usually returned at least once over the Easter holiday but nothing was quite like that first visit; the lights, sounds and smells never seemed the same again. To me it was second only to Christmas morning as the best day of the year.

Dad loved the fair and all that went with it as much as I did. In fact, he used to help Grandpa operate a fairground stall on Hampstead Heath in the 1920s. It was a game stall called 'Cover the Spot'. The aim was to cover a large coloured spot entirely with five smaller discs. The shape and size of the spot and the discs was such that there was only one way the large spot could be covered and, unless you knew the secret, it was almost impossible. To encourage people to part with their money Dad and Grandpa had a little routine worked out. About every half an hour or so, Dad, who was only a young boy then, would wander past as if by chance and Grandpa would shout out to him, 'Sonny, you look like a clever lad! Do you want to have a go?' Dad, who of course knew how it was done, would then complete the puzzle and walk off. Everyone would think that if a young boy could do it then it had to be easy, so they would line up to try it, making Grandpa lots of money as he rarely had to give out any prizes. It was only those who stayed watching for more than half an hour who ever suspected anything odd!

Whenever we won a goldfish, it was given to us inside a small plastic bag full of water. The first time this happened, we had nowhere to put it when we got home so we had to make do with a large dish we had. As soon as we could, we went out and bought a large bowl. We then thought it looked a bit lonely so, the next time Dad went down the Lane, he bought an aquarium and some more goldfish and brought them home on the bus. A little while afterwards, I went to the River Lea to see if I could catch any fish myself to put in the aquarium and managed to catch a few sticklebacks. The next morning, they had all disappeared – we could only assume the goldfish had eaten them.

From this small beginning, we kept fish for many years, topping up our collection at regular intervals with prizes from the fair.

Easter was also the first holiday of the year when John came home, so I was able to spend some time with him. Being a sporty household, we had a number of games we could play. We had a dart board, a small billiards table and we also extended the dining-room table to play table tennis. John and I used to take each other on at all these, though I didn't stand much chance against him. Nevertheless, it was brilliant having my brother home for a while.

On one of his early visits home, he introduced us to the wonders of coffee. We had never had coffee in the house, Mum and Dad always preferring a nice cup of tea, which, of course, in those days was made with real tea leaves – we always had Ty-Phoo – scooped out of the caddy with a teaspoon, one for each person and one for the pot, put into the teapot and boiling water poured over them. The teapot then had a tea cosy placed over it to keep it warm while it was brewing – none of those new-fangled tea bags then. John had discovered coffee at school and persuaded Mum to buy some for the house. His favourite brand was Bev, which was a liquid coffee and chicory essence sold in a bottle. I can't say their first taste impressed Mum and Dad much and, in spite of John's protestations that it was a great new drink, they continued with their tea and left him to finish up the bottle on his own.

The summer holiday was always a good time. Mum would arrange lots of outings to places like Epping Forest, which was only a bus ride away. We used to go to the Rising Sun pub in Woodford, not in it, but in the grounds, because they had a boating lake there and we'd take out a small boat and row round and round the lake until we heard the familiar cry, 'Come in, number seven, your time is up!' Sometimes we went to Whipps Cross lido, which, when it opened in 1932, was the largest open-air swimming pool in the country, with a 20-foot-high diving board, racing lanes and a paddling area. Sadly, it fell into disuse and in 1983 was filled in. I have to say I wasn't much of a fan of the lido as I once cut my foot there and remained a bit wary of it after that.

We always took a picnic with us and would venture a little way into the forest itself to find a clearing where we could have our eats. One day, on returning to the road to catch the bus, Mum got her foot stuck in some mud. She started to panic a bit and I didn't know what to do. I tried tugging at her arm but it didn't do any good and it looked as though we might be trapped there until night-time – I had all sorts of visions of wild animals coming out of the forest and eating us. I got really scared so my poor mum not only had to try to get her foot free but also to calm me down. Eventually, she managed to wriggle her foot out of her shoe. Gosh, was I relieved when I saw her foot squelch out of that mud! The shoe itself was stuck fast and, although we both tried yanking it free, it just sank further in so she had to get on the bus and come back home with just one shoe on and the other foot caked in mud. Goodness knows what the conductor and the other passengers must have thought about this strangely attired woman with the black leg and only the one shoe getting on their bus.

Another fine-weather activity was to go to the putting green at the back of Millfields and play a round. There were also some tennis courts there but we didn't have racquets so we never played. Near to the putting green was an old bandstand surrounded by trees, which often played host to a mobile cinema during the summer. This was a large brown van in which all the cinema equipment was kept. A big screen was set up outside the van and the films projected onto it from the van itself. There was no seating provided and the audience was expected to stand or sit on the ground to watch. Laurel and Hardy shorts were the staple diet. The trees gave some shade but on a very sunny day it was a bit difficult to actually see the flickering black and white films, though that didn't really matter to all the chattering children that flocked to these shows as it was something different, a bit of an occasion and one where you'd get to meet all your school friends again during the holiday.

In the summer, we went a bit further afield for our shopping, travelling by the number 22 bus from the top of Chatsworth Road to Mare Street to visit the big shops, Marks & Spencer, British Home Stores and, best of all, Woolworths. Woolworths was much more my type of shop as it had plenty of toys and other interesting items for sale, unlike M&S and BHS, which only offered clothes. I could spend hours in Woolworths gazing in awe at all the goods they had on offer – skittles and quoits, jigsaws, model cars, toy soldiers, carpentry sets, Meccano, train sets. It was a little boy's paradise, and I loved our visits there. Woolworths also had their own record label, Embassy, which were cover versions of the hits of the day. Occasionally, when we went there, Mum risked Dad's wrath by buying a couple of these, the Embassy versions of two big hits of the day, Tab Hunter's 'Young Love' and Pat Boone's 'April Love'. Given Dad's views on modern music and his insistence that we only have classical music, especially Gilbert and Sullivan, in the house, I thought this was very brave of her but I don't think she ever cared too much what he thought as she was very independently minded in that way.

Mare Street was the place for buying shoes as there were two big shoe shops there, Dolcis and Lilley & Skinner. I always preferred Dolcis because they had an X-ray machine. After trying on a new pair of shoes, you walked over to what looked like a large wooden box, stood up against it, put your feet in a hole at the bottom and looked through what seemed like a pair of binoculars at the top. You then waggled your toes to see how much growing room there was inside each shoe.

The other shop we always visited was Sainsbury's. Like the other grocer shops at the time, it wasn't self-service and you had to go to the counter to ask for what you wanted. But this was much bigger and posher than the shops in Chatsworth Road and looked quite palatial inside, with its marble counters, mosaic floors and white-tiled walls. The staff even wore a uniform. It also had its own cooked meat and cheese counters where we could buy fresh produce. Mum normally bought Summer County margarine to go on our bread, but when we went to Sainsbury's she would buy half a pound of butter as a special little luxury.

It was always a treat for me to see the shop assistant carve out a wodge of butter from a big mound of the stuff they had behind the counter and then pat it out with two grooved wooden paddles into an oblong shape. Although they worked fast, it took them some time as they were at pains to get it exactly right. The butter was then wrapped in greaseproof paper, put in a paper bag and handed to us. When we got it out at home and unwrapped it, the marks of the grooves in the paddles were still very clear.

We also bought sugar from Sainsbury's in loose bags rather than the prepackaged type we got from our local shops. The sugar was scooped up from a large bin, poured into a blue conical bag and then weighed. The top was given a twist and handed over.

Another commodity we always bought on our visits was salt. This came in a large block, which was cut from an even bigger block by the assistant. When we got it home, we had to grate it ourselves into a glass jar. Sometimes I made models out of the salt block – it was very good for snow scenes.

When the weather was not so good, we would go to the cinema, mostly the Plaza in Leyton High Road, to see the cartoons. The Plaza used to put on programmes showing short cartoons, no main feature film, just a number of Mickey Mouse, Goofy, Donald Duck, Bugs Bunny, Woody Woodpecker or Tom & Jerry cartoons plus the obligatory Pearl & Dean advertising feature and Pathé News. We'd also visit other local cinemas if a good film was being shown. Over the years, we saw all the big Disney feature films, such as *Snow White*, *101 Dalmatians* and *Lady and the Tramp*. We also saw the latest 'blockbusters' and perhaps the biggest of these was *Davy Crockett – King of the Wild Frontier*, starring Fess Parker.

Davy Crockett had begun as a very popular television mini-series in the United States but, when the film was produced off the back of it, Disney launched it in a flurry of publicity and marketing to cash in on the UK market as well. There was an enormous merchandising campaign, something we take for granted nowadays with big films, but was quite rare then, and all sorts of toys and clothes were produced to coincide with the premiere, the most iconic being the Davy Crockett coonskin cap. Every boy my age had to have one and, sure enough, when we came out of the cinema I said to Mum, 'Can I have a Davy Crockett cap?' So we stopped off at Woolworths and bought one. I wore it on the way home and for a couple of days it was the envy of my friends until they all bought one as well.

As well as going on days out with Mum, I played with my friends. Quite often, it would be just Andy. Being very keen on sport, we also used to watch Test match cricket on television. I can remember we saw Jim Laker perform his remarkable feat of taking nineteen Australian wickets in the fourth Test of the 1956 Ashes series, a record that still stands to this day. As he bowled out more and more of the Australians, we both got very excited and jumped up and down every time a wicket fell, which is actually more than Laker or the England cricketers were doing. Whenever a wicket fell, there were no celebrations as there would be today. Everyone on the pitch just remained calm and carried on as though nothing was happening. When the innings was over, there were just a couple of handshakes for Laker and that was it. I can't imagine everyone being so restrained today; there'd be mass celebrations, high-fives, everyone surrounding the bowler, thumping him on the back, throwing him up into the air. The bowler himself would probably be jumping about and punching the air and there'd be spectators running onto the pitch. None of that in 1956, but that was cricket in the fifties for you.

As we got a bit older, we started going to see cricket live at Leyton, where Essex played county cricket. At that time, Essex used to play their county cricket all round the county, normally playing two matches at each ground. Today they are mainly based in Chelmsford and, if you want to see them play, you have to go to them rather than have them bring cricket to you.

Being a great lover of sport, I got very excited about a number of other famous sporting occasions. I used to watch the Cup Final on television without fail every year. The first one I saw was the famous Stanley Matthews' final of 1953 when Blackpool beat Bolton 4–3. Matthews had been our finest footballer for a generation but had never won an FA Cup winners' medal. This was the final that changed all that as he played for Blackpool. There was a great outpouring of relief and goodwill towards him as the whole country, no matter what team you supported, felt that justice had at last been done for one of our greatest sporting ambassadors and that he had won the medal he so richly deserved.

Just a month later, there was a similar emotional event when the best jockey in this country, Sir Gordon Richards, won the Derby for the first time on Pinza. He had been champion jockey many times since his first win in 1925 but had never managed to win horse racing's greatest prize, the Derby. As his horse came over the line, the crowd went frantic and to thunderous applause he was led up to be personally congratulated by HM the Queen. Like Matthews, he was feted throughout the country as everyone it seemed was relieved and pleased that he had at last achieved his greatest ambition.

The following year, 1954, was the year Roger Bannister broke the famous four-minute barrier for the mile at the Iffley Road track in Oxford. For years, this had been the Holy Grail for athletes and I was lucky enough to see this on television as well. I can still remember Bannister finishing absolutely exhausted and falling into the arms of his friend, the Revd. Nicholas Stacey, unable to move another inch. Nowadays, four minutes is commonplace and anyone doing it in that time would have no problem in trotting off to the changing room unaided. But then it was one of sport's major achievements and, even though I was only six at the time, I could not fail to recognise its significance.

There were many other great sporting events I saw on television or heard on the wireless, such as the Jaroslav Drobny and Ken Rosewall Wimbledon Men's Tennis Final in 1954, the first time a Brit won motor racing's British Grand Prix when Stirling Moss took the chequered flag in 1955 at Aintree and the Don Cockell/Rocky Marciano fight for the World Heavyweight Championship in 1956. These were all larger-than-life characters and events that, in a world without computers or social media, only came along once in a while, and you had to be there or miss them – and I was usually there.

A shared love of sport meant that Andy and I also played a number of games based on cricket and football. Our favourite was a cricket game, Owzthat. This was played with two six-sided metal cylinders. One was labelled 1, 2, 3, 4, 'owzthat' and 6, while the second was labelled bowled, stumped, caught, not out, no ball and L.B.W. Usually, we played the game as two Test teams, so that one of us would be England and the other whichever team was touring that year. Whoever was 'batting' started by rolling the batting cylinder; any runs scored were written down on our homemade scorecard. When 'owzthat' appeared, the other cylinder was rolled for the decision. The 'batsman' was out if 'bowled', 'stumped', 'caught' or 'L.B.W.' appeared and so on until ten players were out and the other team went in to bat.

I also played this game quite a bit on my own and tried to get through a whole county championship season. It certainly taught me the names of the county cricketers in the 1950s.

The football games we played most were blow football, magnetic football and Newfooty, which was a forerunner of Subbuteo and almost identical. But the highlight of the school summer holiday was undoubtedly the week or two weeks when we went away to the seaside…

CHAPTER SIX

BUTLIN'S, WARNER'S AND CLACTON PIER

My first ever holiday away from home and first experience of the seaside came when the four of us stayed at Butlin's Holiday Camp in Clacton. Dad had been stationed in Clacton during the War, so he wanted to see what it was like during peacetime. I was three when we first went there and we followed this up by spending our annual holidays there every year until 1955.

Holiday camps and Butlin's in particular became enormously popular in the late 1940s and 1950s. One of the main attractions was the fact that you paid your money to go to the camp for a week and everything was laid on for you: accommodation, food, entertainment, amusements and games. In theory, you could go to the camp with no money at all in your pocket and still have a really good time so it was a boon to most working-class families, many of them never having had a proper holiday before. Though, in fact, it wasn't just a working-class pursuit, as plenty of middle-class people took advantage of their facilities as well. In a society still very much class-ridden, the holiday camps did much to break down barriers as solicitors joined in the sports with lorry drivers, head teachers ate their meals next to factory workers and bank managers danced in the Viennese Ballroom alongside bus conductors. For one week in the year, everyone was equal; everyone could have fun together. And for women especially, and possibly for the first time in their lives, it was a week away from the drudgery of housekeeping. There was no cooking to do, no cleaning and no beds to make.

Billy Butlin spared no expense to give the people what they wanted in the hope that they would return again and again. He laid on top-class entertainment, and my parents went to the on-site theatres in the evening to see shows and performers ranging from the popular entertainers of the day such as Gracie Fields and Maurice Fogel to opera, ballet and Shakespeare. Butlin also arranged for top-class sports stars to coach the campers. One year when I was there, the cricket coach for the season was none other than Maurice Tate, the former Sussex fast bowler who had played in thirty-nine Test matches for England.

There was something special about a holiday at Butlin's as for just one week of the year you could let your hair down in austerity-hit Britain and really let yourself go and forget the worries of everyday life.

We travelled by coach rather than train as it was easier for us. Also, we were able to introduce a bit of variety into this by catching a different coach each year. These included Grey

Green, Classique, Fallowfield and Britten and one year a coach
sadly misnamed Orange Luxury, which was probably the most
uncomfortable ride we ever had the misfortune to suffer in
an old boneshaker of a coach. We had to go in the school
holidays, firstly because of John and later because of me as
well, so it was very busy on the roads going down there and
we always spent a good deal of our travelling time stuck in a
mammoth traffic jam at the infamous Marks Tey roundabout.
At that time, the A12 only contained one small piece of dual
carriageway somewhere near Chelmsford. It was very wide and
had trees growing in the middle. Now, of course, the whole
of the A12 is dual carriageway from the Blackwall Tunnel in
London to Great Yarmouth and the Marks Tey roundabout has
been relegated to a fairly minor role.

When we arrived at the camp, we were greeted by the jolly
redcoats – 'Hi-de-hi!' – and given our chalet key and badge at
reception. The redcoats were mostly young hopeful entertainers,
a number of whom went on to become very famous. I can
remember seeing the young comedian Jack Douglas and the
singer Michael Holliday there before they went on to bigger
and better things.

You had to wear the badge to let you back into the camp past
the gate security guard if you'd been out for the day. We were
also allocated to one of the 'houses' of which there were two,
Gloucester and Kent. The idea of being in a house was that
every time you entered any of the laid-on sports and games,
whether it was a team sport like football or cricket, or an
individual event such as table tennis or snooker, you could win
points for your house and at the end of the week the captain

of the house with the most points would go up and receive the trophy for that week in a special ceremony on the last evening. But it wasn't just sports that could win you points because this was also the era of the knobbly knees, glamorous grandmother, Tarzan lookalike and spaghetti-eating competitions. Often we would go and watch these events, though we didn't ever take part. Dad wasn't one for exerting any effort on holiday and used his week away for relaxing as much as possible. But he did like watching what he called 'all-for-its'. These were the people who went in for absolutely everything: the football team, the cricket team, the swimming, the knobbly knees, the spaghetti eating. You name it, they were in it! They knew how to enjoy a holiday.

In the last year we were there, at breakfast on our final day, the waitress said to John, 'Well done, you were very unlucky last night.' Apparently, he had lost in the final of the table tennis competition. He was fifteen at the time but had said nothing about it to any of us. This was the first we knew he had even been in the competition, let alone reached the final.

I used to enjoy going in the free funfair, where my favourite ride was the 'Peter Pan' railway with its little engines wending their way round a twisty track. There was also a miniature railway that went all the way round the camp, which was another very enjoyable ride. I also have fond memories of the swimming pool with its sparkling blue, white and cream-coloured fountain, so cool on a hot sunny day as, of course, every day was in everyone's childhood. It was at Butlin's that I finally learnt to swim. I can remember one day I walked out to the middle of the pool at the shallow end and announced with great confidence that I would swim the half a width back. For what seemed like ages, I swam and swam with my arms and legs flailing about, getting absolutely nowhere. Although I had managed to stay afloat I had actually only moved forward about an inch.

Although our holidays at Butlin's were normally very enjoyable, I did have one very bad day the last year we were there. I was eight at the time and Mum and Dad thought I should join the Beaver Club. This was a club that laid on many activities for young children during the day and gave the parents some peace and quiet, as well as time to themselves. On this particular morning, the Beaver Club had arranged a nature walk around the camp and in the immediate vicinity outside. My parents left me with the group and went off. I started out on the walk but I wasn't very interested and really wanted to be with Mum and Dad, so I sneaked away and went looking for them on the beach. I walked all along the prom up to the main centre of Clacton, a distance of about one mile, looking down at the beach to see if I could see them, but I couldn't so I walked all the way back again. By the time I returned to the camp, I was in tears because I thought I'd lost them. However, when I got back to the chalet they were there. Was I pleased to see them! They could both see how upset I was and Dad took a quick look at the day's programme (Butlin's used to issue a weekly programme with all the events for each day on it) and saw there was an 'Indian Pow Wow' just starting on the Playing Fields. This was another event aimed mainly at children, though this time parents could stay with them, so he said, 'Come on, let's go and see what this is all about.' While walking there, I got stung by a wasp. More tears – it just wasn't my day.

As well as the camp itself, there was Clacton as a town. It was a relatively new town, having been founded only eighty years previously by a man called Peter Bruff, whose sole intention had been to create a seaside resort on the Essex coast. Clacton therefore put everything into enticing visitors so that plenty of amusements and entertainments grew up over the years. Its closeness to London made it an ideal destination for holidaymakers, particularly from the East End of London, and in the 1950s, before the advent of cheap package holidays abroad, it was still one of the country's leading seaside resorts.

The first attraction we came across after leaving the camp was the donkeys. There was a little grass enclosure where they took children for a ride round an elliptical course. My favourite donkey was Daisy and I always tried to get a ride on her whenever we went there. She wasn't there one year and so I had to ride on Doris instead – it just wasn't the same.

We often went and sat out on the beach, where Dad's attempts at opening up the deck chairs would usually cause Mum and me great amusement as he never could get the hang of it. But once this ordeal (for him) was over, he'd sit back and relax with his knotted handkerchief on his head to keep off the sun. I loved making sandcastles and paddling in the sea, usually with Mum, who might even go in for a bit of swimming. I once asked Dad how sand was made and he replied over thousands of years the stones would be worn down by the sea into little grains of sand. Every time we went onto the beach after that, I kept picking up stones and asking him how long it would be before this particular stone became a grain of sand. Looking back, I expect this must have been very irritating but he bore it with

Above left: My earliest photo, showing my shock of thick black hair.

Above right: John in front our prefab, No. 7 Millfield Terrace.

Below left: Mum in the back garden with the field behind.

Below right: Dad in the front garden with the main entrance to Clapton Greyhound Stadium just beyond, showing how close we were.

Above left: Our first rent card, showing a total weekly rent of 16s 8d.

Above right: Mum behind Copper and Bally's prefabs.

Below left: Dad and Mum standing on the field just in front of our prefab. This gives an indication of how far the prefabs were set back from Millfields Road. In the background on the left is Old Daddy Flat Cap's pride and joy.

Below right: The bill for our first television, signed by none other than Mr H. G. Lassman himself.

Above left: Dad in our kitchen. On the left is the sink he bathed me in when Mum had gone out to give me my earliest memory.

Above right: On Arabella, my favourite push-along toy. In the background you can just make out the old bandstand.

Below left: With my box of toys on the side path. In the background is the shed housing the coal bin – famous for its Catherine wheel displays!

Below right: Spot the cat relaxing in the garden.

Left: My invitation to the Coronation Party at the Glyn Road Mission.

Right: Riding my tricycle in the Coronation procession along Millfields Road while Dad looks on proudly.

Left: A corner of Rushmore Road Junior School. The door on the right at the top of the small flight of stairs was one of those I could never find from the inside.

Right: Home time! Rushmore Road Infants' School.

Above: Our group of seven at a Christmas party at Rushmore Road School (*back row left to right*): unknown, me, Johnnie Walker, Peter Hannaford, Bob Marriott, Howard Bradbury, Andy Shalders, Terry Gregory.

Below: Dad arriving home from work. Over the road is Pete's off-licence, the Chippendale Arms. Right from there are the residences of Ginger, the woman no one talked about, the Laneys and the Gatewallers.

Above left: John demonstrating the art of cricket to me – though I seem more interested in playing football…

Above right: Off to play cricket on the field with the back entrance to the Greyhound Stadium behind.

Below left: Aunt Clara, Grandpa and Nanny Jacobs on Christmas Day in the prefab.

Below right: With Mum and Nanny Sinnott in our back garden.

Top: Arthur Toms Pie 'n' Mash shop closed in c. 1973/4 and a Chinese restaurant opened up in its place. When I visited Chatsworth Road in 2012, the restaurant had closed and the new owners were stripping back the frontage, revealing Arthur Toms. You can just make out 'LIVE EELS' written in the glass of the right-hand window.

Above left: Dad, Mum and me outside our Butlin's chalet in 1955.

Below right: Our first car, Arnold Pentecost, arriving at Nanny's in Chingford Hatch.

Top: 1A at Parmiter's. I am at the back right. Just in front of me to the right is Murray Glickman. John Hill is far left on the front row, while Herbert Tyler is directly behind him, and Bob Marriott immediately to the right of Herbert. Our form teacher, Mr Blake, is in the centre of the front row.

Above left: All ready for Parmiter's!

Above right: Dad and me after our historic ride on the world's first commercial hovercraft service.

Left: My programme from the ill-fated Del Shannon concert at the Walthamstow Granada, which I went to see with Minna.

good humour and always gave me an answer, '20,000 years', '5,000 years' or whatever he thought might be appropriate.

One thing he didn't bear with good humour, though, was the time we decided to walk into town rather than go onto the beach. The way into the centre of Clacton along Marine Parade passed an old entertainment complex built in 1906 called 'The Palace'. By the 1950s, it had been reduced to just an amusement arcade. Standing at its entrance was a machine called 'Sidney Knows', the upper half consisting of a typical ventriloquist's dummy behind a glass case with a tray underneath on which you placed a penny and pushed it into the machine. On receiving the penny, Sidney would speak and the machine would cough out a card with his words printed on it, usually some trite little aphorism dressed up as a mystical prediction for the future.

One day I decided to try this out and placed my penny in the slot. Nothing. Not a dicky bird came from Sidney's mouth and no card issued forth. I told Dad and he gave the machine a good shaking. Still no luck, so he decided to give it a good kicking. But this didn't work either. And what was worse was that the penny was not returned. He then took hold of the tray and bent it upwards so it was unusable. Satisfied with that, he looked at me and said, 'Well, at least no one else will be rooked by Sidney.' He could, of course, have told someone in the arcade but Dad was a man of action and I think he got far more pleasure out of duffing up the machine than he would have done by just reporting it and getting his penny back.

The Pier was situated at the town end. Almost as good as Butlin's itself, there were plenty of rides to go on, my favourite being the Steel Stella roller coaster, which was very exciting, especially the first drop when my heart leapt into my mouth and the breath seemed to be wrenched out of me. Looking at old footage of it now, it seems very tame compared to what you might find these days at places like Alton Towers or Thorpe Park. Another favourite ride was the Helter Skelter, known as the Cresta Run. The Pier was also the place to buy candy floss. It was an amazing experience to see the sugar being thrown into the machine and watch its transformation into the pink delicacy as the man wound it round and round a stick, then handed it over when it was finished. That candy floss sometimes seemed as big as me and was just about the most exquisite food a young boy could ever put into his mouth, where it would melt away, leaving its sticky remains all over my face.

Next to the Pier were three pleasure boats, *The Viking Saga*, *Nemo II* and *The Jill*, plying their trade sailing up and down just off the coast. We always went on at least one during our holiday. *Nemo II* was the best, as partway through the journey the captain would allow children to have a go on the wheel and steer the boat. One year I was doing this and I thought we were drifting perilously close to the land so I turned the wheel hard to get us back out to sea. When I explained what I'd done to Mum and Dad, Dad said with a straight face, 'It was a good job you were there, we might have crashed otherwise.' I felt very proud.

If we went into the centre of Clacton itself, my favourite place to go was one of the amusement arcades. The best game there was the horse racing game. Up to eighteen players could take part. On the wall in front was a large board displaying the racecourse with the eighteen horses. Each player had one of the numbered horses and sat in front of a board with holes in and a large ball. The players rolled their balls into the target holes, which were numbered from one to four – the number of the hole your ball rolled into was the number of paces your horse moved forwards. It could also miss altogether so your horse wouldn't move at all. The winner won a prize, or you could stay on and try to win again. And the more wins you got, the bigger the prize.

Another favourite was the much simpler 'Allwin' machine, though actually hardly anyone won. This consisted of a fairly small case containing a spiral track and a number of cups, some with numbers on, on top of a wooden stand. The player had to insert a coin in the slot at the top right-hand side of the case; this released a ball inside the machine, which fell onto a spring-loaded hammer at the bottom right. Using all your skill and judgement, you then had to fire the ball by means of a trigger on the outside of the case. This shot the ball up and around the spiral tracks. If the ball fell into one of the cups with a number, you had to turn a knob at the bottom of the case and the machine then paid out the appropriate number of pennies. Most times the ball went right round the spiral and fell through a hole at the bottom, which won you nothing.

There were a number of other machines I liked, including the cranes, pinball machines and football games, which I played with John or Dad. The fact that there were so many machines led me to name the places 'Machine Shops' rather than amusement arcades, and that's how they were always known in our family. On one occasion, we were there on early closing day (yes, even seaside towns had an early closing day at that time) and they were shutting up. The particular machine shop we were in, Marshall's, had a large iron shutter, which they were already bringing down as we were walking towards the exit. I panicked, thinking we might be locked in, and ran for the exit. Mum and Dad continued at their normal pace. When they got outside, Dad said to me, 'You're a nice fellah, aren't you? Running out and leaving us in there!' It was only then that it suddenly struck me that things could have been worse and I might have got out but they could have been locked inside. Only an ice cream cornet could console me.

In town we looked round the shops, particularly Woolworths and Timothy White's and Taylor's, as well as a couple of small toy shops. It was very rare that I came back from a trip into Clacton without some small toy. In spite of the fact that we got all the food we could ever hope for in Butlin's, we usually stopped off for morning or afternoon tea at one of the many cafés and restaurants; Davey's and Cordy's are two I remember in particular.

Walking back to the camp, we would suddenly be assailed by the delicious smell of doughnuts being made. This smell emanated from a small stall not far from the gates of Butlin's itself. It was very difficult to avoid the temptation of buying some hot out of the fryer. Those holidays were non-stop eating!

After our sixth year in Clacton, we decided to be a bit more adventurous and go further afield for our holiday. We still went by coach and always to a holiday camp, though mostly to Warner's rather than Butlin's, starting first with Dovercourt Bay, the camp where the television sitcom *Hi-de-Hi!* was filmed.

This time we went with Nan, Grandpa and Aunt Clara, but it wasn't so good as it didn't have anything like the facilities or the laid-on activities of Butlin's.

Aunt Clara got herself into trouble with the rest of us, but especially Nan, when she volunteered to judge the children's fancy dress competition. We all felt that the girl dressed as a television OMO commercial should win. She wore a large, box-shaped dress in the form of an OMO laundry packet with a television aerial sticking up from it. We all thought it was a very well-executed and original idea that must have taken quite a bit of ingenuity and work on the part of her parents. However, the winner was another girl just dressed in her pyjamas, representing the hit musical *The Pajama Game*, which had recently opened on stage in London.

When Clara returned to us from her seat with the judges, Nan said to her, 'What the bloody hell was all that about? I hope you didn't vote for that pyjama girl.'

Clara replied rather sheepishly that she had and Nan really went off on one – 'She was just wearing her bloody pyjamas! What sort of bloody fancy dress is that? What about the OMO girl? She knocked your winner into a cocked hat.'

In the face of this onslaught, my aunt simply said, 'You wouldn't understand – it's a modern thing.'

Of course, that didn't help and Nan was off again: 'Too right I don't bloody understand,' she bawled. 'All that bloody work that girl and her parents must have put in and you give the prize to a girl who's just wearing her normal bloody pyjamas!'

Aunt Clara didn't comment further, but she and Nan refused to speak to each other for the rest of the day. There was a very frosty atmosphere and all over a bloody fancy dress competition, as Nan would no doubt have put it.

In the following two years, we went even further afield to the Warner camps of Corton in Suffolk, Ryde on the Isle of Wight and finally Seaton in faraway Devon. On these occasions, it was just Mum, Dad and me. After our experience with Nan and Aunt Clara in Dovercourt, we never went with them again and John was now too old to want to come on holiday with his parents any more. By the time I left Junior School, we had certainly got the bug for travelling, which was to intensify even more over the next few years once we'd bought our first car.

CHAPTER SEVEN

JELLY AND
ICE CREAM

THE CORONATION

The earliest special day I can remember was the Coronation of Queen Elizabeth II. I was just four years old when King George VI died, and it is my earliest memory of a national news story. Mum and I were visiting Dad's sister, Aunt Julie, Uncle Isaac and their four children, my cousins, Wendy, Rita, John and Carol, who also lived in a prefab, in Bethnal Green. I can still clearly remember Uncle Isaac coming home from work, throwing the door open to announce loudly, 'The King is dead.' Actually, looking back on it, I'm amazed I understood as he was Scottish and spoke with a very broad accent; most times I couldn't understand a word he said. I always wondered how Aunt Julie managed. Obviously, on this occasion, he must have put on his poshest voice, owing to the momentous news

143

he had to impart. On our way back to the bus stop to go home, I saw the evening newspaper placards (*Star*, *News* and *Standard*) all carrying the same news.

This, of course, was in February 1952. The Coronation of Queen Elizabeth II didn't take place until June 1953, by which time I was six. For weeks beforehand, preparations were being made and by the time the big day arrived our street was full of flags and pennants flying from every house and stuck up in every window. We had a couple of very large Union Jacks in our windows, together with some other bunting around the prefab.

On the day itself, the first thing that happened was a children's party, beginning at 9.30am in the Glyn Road Mission Hall, which was acting as the headquarters for the local festivities. There were long tables covered with white sheets laid out in the hall. The food wasn't particularly stunning as this was still an age of austerity and some food was still on ration (though households were given an extra pound of sugar and four ounces of margarine especially for the celebrations). But in spite of the fact that all we had were fish paste and cucumber sandwiches, sausage rolls, sliced hard-boiled eggs, crisps and jelly and trifle with evaporated milk, along with gallons of orange squash, the whole atmosphere made it seem like a banquet – a veritable queen's feast, as you might say. The excitement and noise of hundreds of children enjoying themselves got the day off to the perfect start.

Following this, there was a children's procession, where we walked or rode on our suitably adorned bicycles, tricycles and scooters around the local streets. I still have a photograph of me riding down Millfields Road with Dad proudly looking on.

After the procession, there was a break in proceedings to allow people to go and watch the Coronation itself on television. We were still one of the few families in the street to have a television so we could watch it at home. Many others went to the big television screen specially set up in the Mission Hall. My aunt Nell, who lived in Blackburn, came all the way down to visit us just so she could see the Coronation on television. At one point, I stood in front of her, blocking her view. I can still remember her saying, 'Could you move your body please, Norman?' It sounded such a strange thing to say to me – I had never quite heard the word 'body' used in that way before.

For the afternoon, a big outdoor gathering was arranged on Millfields with lots of events for children and adults. There were a number of races arranged for the children, which were divided up into under-sevens, under-sixes, under-fives, etc. I believe the cut-off point for entry was 1 May, so that, if you were under six on 1 May, you entered the under-sixes and so on. As it happened, I was under six on 1 May, but by Coronation Day I'd had my sixth birthday. Dad entered me for the under-sixes and told me I had a good chance of winning since I would be one of the oldest in the race. However, I wanted to be a big boy and didn't want to enter the under-sixes so I told him I wanted to enter the under-sevens. Reluctantly, he agreed and when the race came I finished nowhere as, of course, I was now the youngest of the competitors. My chance to redeem myself came with the egg and spoon race and I was doing so well in second place until I dropped my egg just on the line. I managed to pick it up, but sadly could only finish fourth.

After the sports, the prize-giving ceremony for all those who had done well took place in the Mission Hall. Dad said, 'There's not much point in us going to that,' but I clung onto the faint hope that there might be prizes given out for fourth place in the egg and spoon race, so we went along. Of course, only the first three received prizes. Still, we didn't go away empty-handed as we were all given a goody bag to take home, which included a book with a souvenir coin attached to the front as well as some other souvenirs and sweets. I still have the book, and I cherish the memory of that day.

REMEMBER, REMEMBER THE FIFTH OF NOVEMBER

Preparations for Guy Fawkes Night started some months before the big day as I used to start paying 6d a week into 'Funny Eye's' Fireworks Club. 'Funny Eye' was the name us children unkindly gave to the owner of a stationery shop in Chatsworth Road. The sign above the shop proclaimed her real name was A. E. Barrow, but she had a squint in one eye, hence our name for her. The idea was that you'd pay whatever you could afford for two or three months and on 5 November you would be presented with a box of fireworks to the value of however much you had paid in. There was no choice about what you got, other than being able to specify 'no bangers' if you wanted to, for which I was thankful. Bangers seemed a waste of money to me, as all they did was go bang.

About two weeks before the big day, Mum and I made up our guy with old clothes and other bits and pieces ready to sit on top of our bonfire. Living next door to Clapton dogs,

I had a captive market for the 'Penny for the guy' routine. I used to take it down to the bottom of the path and sit with the guy on Thursday and Saturday evenings as the thousands of punters passed by on their way in. Sometimes I was joined by Barry and Richard from along the prefabs and we would share the proceeds.

I must have been seven when I first sat out with my guy and, every time someone gave me more than a penny, I got so excited that I ran back up the path, shouting, 'Mum, Mum, someone's just given me a shilling!' Unbeknownst to me, Mum was dying of embarrassment. Eventually, after the third or fourth such excursion, she said, 'Stop doing that! We don't want people to think we're beggars.' I have to say the greyhound fraternity were quite generous and for just a couple of weeks a year this was a lucrative pastime.

On firework night itself, I used to help Dad build the bonfire in our back garden. The wood was easy to come by as we just used to pick up fallen branches from the field.

For some reason now lost in the mists of time, our traditional tea on bonfire night was liver and bacon, after which we would all go out in the garden and light the bonfire. Dad used to supplement my 'firework club' fireworks with another box or two, usually made by Brocks or Pains as we always considered theirs to be the best. Once the bonfire was truly ablaze, Dad would start lighting the fireworks. The rockets were placed in a milk bottle, which in those days had long necks, so they could shoot skywards unimpeded from their improvised launchpad. Other favourites were Roman Candles, Golden Rain (which could be held in a gloved hand), Sparklers (ditto) and Mount

Vesuvius (very bright and lit everything up like daylight). Less popular were the coloured sparklers, which were supposed to give off a red, blue or green colour, but usually just emitted clouds of smoke, and Arora, which didn't seem to do much at all except make a crackling noise that sounded like liver and bacon frying. This may well have been the origin of our traditional tea.

Our greatest love/hate relationship was reserved for the Catherine Wheel. Dad pinned them to the shed door, gave them a flip to make sure they would spin freely and then lit the blue touchpaper. This was supposed to result in them spinning round, emitting a spectacular rainbow of colours. At least that was according to the instructions. Actually, I can't remember one single occasion when this happened. Most times they wouldn't move at all and the sparks just sprayed out from a stationary wheel, usually straight at the ground. Occasionally, just occasionally, it would move slightly but never as far as a whole circle. In spite of Dad risking his hand by giving the wheel some manual help, it was the same every year. Why we thought it might be different I can't imagine.

While the big fireworks were going off, we lit up the hand-held ones and sometimes danced round the bonfire, singing, 'Guy, Guy, Guy/Punch him in the eye/Hang him on a lamppost/And there let him die'. This was a song Mum said she remembered from her childhood. The violent nature of it seems all the more odd coming from Mum's childhood and her family, considering they were an Irish Roman Catholic family.

Where we lived in Clapton, there were no large organised displays, but most of the prefabs had bonfires and fireworks of their own. On one occasion, Bertha and David next door got their bonfire going and then undid a packet of giant sparklers. David lit one and came over to the fence holding it proudly aloft, exclaiming loudly and with great glee, 'You can't beat me!' This phrase passed into our family folklore as one we would use ourselves when we did something we thought was good.

Although the prefab gardens were quite spacious, the bonfires and fireworks were nevertheless in close proximity to the houses. I'm sure that any modern-day fire prevention officer or health & safety officer would have an apoplectic fit if these events happened now.

CHRISTMAS

There was a short lull after Bonfire Night before preparations for the next big day began in earnest. That big day was, of course, Christmas Day.

The first weekend in December was our traditional day for putting up the decorations, though I would have spent some time beforehand making paper chains with Mum. There were some shop-bought decorations as well but pride of place naturally went to our own paper chains.

We also had a real Christmas tree to decorate every year. I don't know where it came from but Dad always turned up with it on the Friday before the first weekend. It must have been some feat getting it home on the bus, but the logistics involved in this never occurred to me at the time.

Once the decorations were up and the tree decorated with the familiar battered baubles and fairy, there was a short lull interrupted only by a number of presents mysteriously appearing under the tree. Strangely enough, in my younger days these were all left by Father Christmas, but later on were left by my parents.

Once school broke up for the holiday, the excitement and expectation became tangible. Every year Mum would take me up to London on the bus. We always made for Gamages first. Gamages was a big department store in Holborn and a bit out of the main West End shopping centre around Oxford Street. Although situated in an unfashionable shopping area, it was a mecca for children because of its unparalleled stock of toys. One of its main attractions was a large working model railway, which alternated between a day and night scene by the use of lighting. There was also a large Meccano exhibition every year, with some of the exhibits being driven by little model steam engines.

Another attraction for me was the way the whole store was set out. It had been started in 1878 by Arthur Walter Gamage in one small unit, but as the business prospered and expanded it took over all the shops around it until it occupied a whole block (nos 116–128 Holborn). Because of its piecemeal expansion, it ended up as a maze of rooms, steps, passages and ramps because the floors were on slightly different levels. It was a real adventure wandering through this warren and you felt as though you were in a place straight out of a Grimms' Fairy Tale. Not for nothing was it known as the People's Popular Emporium.

Gamages also still used the old vacuum tube system for payments, which necessitated a jumble of wires and tubes overhead. When you bought something, you would give the sales assistant behind the counter the money for payment and they would make out a receipt. The receipt and money would then be put into a cylindrical container with a screw cap. This in turn would be placed in a tube. At the pull of a cord, a bell would ding, and, with a whoosh of air, the cylinder, by magic, would be transported along the wires to the cashier situated centrally in an office on the floor. The cashier then took the receipt and the cash out of the tube, checked it was correct, and, if necessary, supplied the change. She then signed the receipt and sent it all back again. It was a bit of a laborious process but still wonderful to see the tubes whishing backwards and forwards across the store. Somehow it all added to the magic of Gamages.

As well as just the general air of the place and the vast stock of toys, we went for two specific purposes. The first, of course, was to see Father Christmas. Every year there would be a different theme to his grotto, but the main thing was being able to tell him what you wanted for Christmas and then getting a small present on the way out. The second was to have our 'Cracker Tea'. This consisted of a cup of tea for Mum, orange squash for me, some cakes to share and a cracker for us to pull. Yes, a visit to Gamages was definitely one of the highlights of Christmas.

After spending some time in Gamages, we would get the bus up to Selfridges on Oxford Street to see Father Christmas again, this time with his sidekick, Mr Holly. I don't think it ever struck me as strange that Santa could be in two places at once – I suppose I must have reasoned that if we could get from one store to the other so could he. Perhaps he got the bus up, like we did. As at Gamages, I sat on his knee, told him what I wanted for Christmas and received a small gift. I always preferred Gamages' Santa, though, because he seemed jollier and gave better presents. Also, I didn't like Mr Holly. To me he seemed a bit creepy.

There was a third Father Christmas we sometimes visited, though not every year, and that was the one in Dudley's, a big department store in Dalston. He wasn't as good as Gamages' Father Christmas either. This was partly because, being in Dalston, it didn't seem like much of an adventure as we sometimes went there to do shopping at other times of the year as well. There was no fancy grotto either, just Santa sitting on a chair in the toy department. And there was just no magic about Dudley's Father Christmas. His presents weren't as good either. The only thing going for Dudley's was that it too used the vacuum tube system for payment.

After the visit to the big shops, there were still a few days to wait. I would make out my list for Father Christmas, though I think he already had a good idea what I wanted from conversations I'd had with my parents! The list was duly posted to Santa at his Lapland workshop and then all I had to do was wait for the big day itself. Final preparations were made on Christmas Eve, the most important of which was hanging up my stocking. I also made sure that a mince pie and glass of orange squash were left out on the table for Santa, as well as a carrot for Rudolph the reindeer as this might induce them to leave me an extra present.

After what seemed an eternity, Christmas Day finally arrived. Up at the crack of dawn to my full stocking with presents strewn all over the bed, I often wondered how Santa had sneaked them in without waking me up. I'd take everything into Mum and Dad's room and open it all up there.

I'm not sure how old I was but one year there was a very strange present. Well, the present itself wasn't that strange; it was a game that had six plastic crows on a wire and a pop gun you fired at the crows to try to knock them off the wire. What *was* strange was that written on the wrapping paper were the words 'To Norman with love from Grandpa'. Now this was a bit strange. Why would Father Christmas be leaving me a present from Grandpa? As it happens, it was that Christmas that my parents had decided they would tell me the truth about Santa Claus but it didn't come as a great shock as I'd already worked it out, thanks to Grandpa!

After opening the bedroom presents and leaving a mountain of paper behind, it was into the big room to open the presents under the Christmas tree. When that was done, it was probably still only about 8am, if that. So, breakfast was next up and then the morning was spent playing with the new toys, while, every alternate year, Mum and Dad started getting dinner ready. I say every alternate year because one year we would entertain Nanny, Grandpa, Aunt Clara and Uncle Bob, while the next year we would go there. Fortunately for us, in those days, buses ran a Sunday service on Christmas Day so you could still get around.

When it was our turn, there would always be a turkey for Christmas lunch. I can't remember how the tradition started but for some obscure reason, and in keeping with his penchant for nicknames, Dad always called the turkey Louis. By the time we left the prefab in 1965, I think we were on for something like

Louis XVIII. As well as turkey, there were all the usual trimmings, roast and mashed potatoes, Brussels sprouts, cauliflower and so on. As my family rarely drank, there would normally be Tizer to accompany the meal. This was followed by the Christmas pudding, though we never had any silver threepenny bits or silver charms inside, unlike some of my friends.

The Christmas pudding took days to make. Mum would mix up the ingredients one day then let it stand for another day before steaming it in the copper for at least eight hours. It was then left until Christmas Day, when it was put back in the copper for another couple of hours before serving.

The afternoon was given over to various games. One of our favourites was a game called Escalado. The game involved having five metal horses placed at the start line of a track. Each member of the family was able to bet on a horse, with one player acting as the bookie. The horses were then moved by the bookie by turning a mechanical hand crank that vibrated the entire track in a random fashion such that it would simulate the events of a live race. The track also had several lines of small bumps across it, which could either block a horse's progress or even make it fall.

It was through this game that I learnt the rudiments of betting. I was acting as bookie for one race and, as one horse had continually performed worse than all the others, I think I gave it odds of ten to one. Dad said, 'You can't do that! There's only six of us betting, so if someone bets on it and it wins you'll lose money. You can't make it any more than four to one.'

This made sense to me but also destroyed a lot of interest in the game as it meant the odds of the five horses were all bunched together around evens or odds on. I knew that real horses had odds of 100/1!

During the games, everyone would tuck into sweets, dates, figs and all the usual Christmas fare, while I'd eat the tangerine and apple from my stocking. Even though we were continually nibbling something all afternoon, games were followed by tea and telly. Tea was usually turkey sandwiches or there was always smoked salmon if you felt like a rest from turkey.

Although my family rarely drank alcohol, the evening did see some ginger wine and Eggnog or Snowball being consumed. It was the only time all year that I ever saw Dad drink. In fact, one of his presents every year was a bottle of ginger wine. Even at Christmas Mum didn't drink – she said it made her legs 'go all funny'.

My grandparents had to leave reasonably early to catch the last bus back to Chingford Hatch but not before the highlight of every Christmas, the reciting of the old poetic melodrama *Little Nell*. There were parts in it for everyone and everyone knew their part. It began:

'Twas a dark and stormy night when me Nelly went away.
I'll never forget her till my dying day.
She was just sixteen and the village queen,
The prettiest little trick that the village had seen.

It went on to tell the heart-rending and poignant tale of Little Nell, who was made pregnant by the villain of the piece and then abandoned on the night her little 'Dumbell' was born. However, everything turns out well in the end as the villain gets his comeuppance by being fined 'a dollar and a quarter'.

After my grandparents and aunt and uncle had gone, there was a bit more telly for us and then bed after a very long and busy day.

The following day, Boxing Day, we would do it all in reverse, with us visiting Chingford. Mum never saw her family over Christmas. Although Dad was a great believer in family, I think he took this to mean the Jacobs family! Boxing Day followed a similar pattern as far as the visit went, though Nan always had a capon for dinner rather than a turkey. One year, when I was about nine or ten, she had a goose, which for me was a completely novel experience as I'd never had it before. I found it very fatty and wished she'd stuck to the capon!

BIRTHDAYS

In some ways, birthdays were like a mini-Christmas except that they were celebrated more with friends than my family. There was the eager anticipation and the thought of receiving presents together with a party. As my birthday is in May, it was also nice to have this to look forward to about halfway between Christmases.

I can't remember having a birthday at the weekend, so they all occurred on a school day. The day would start with the usual getting ready for school but with the difference that there would be some cards to open. Mum and Dad's would be on the kitchen table ready for when I got there for breakfast and there might also be some that had arrived by post. During the 1950s, we had three posts a day and our first one arrived very early, usually before I left for school. I could normally count on receiving cards from John and from my grandparents and sometimes my uncles and aunts if they remembered. When they did remember, these usually contained a postal order for 2/6d or, if I was lucky, sometimes for as much as five shillings.

The school day passed very slowly as I was always eager to get back home, where Mum had laid on a birthday party for me and my friends – the usual six. Sometimes, under a bit of pressure from my parents, I would invite a couple of girls as I think they thought it would make us behave a bit better and be less rowdy. It never did, though, as I made sure that the girls I invited were the ones who liked to play boys' games – especially Judith, who I don't remember ever seeing in a skirt or dress. She always wore blue jeans and loved playing football. As far as we were concerned, she was an honorary boy, but there was no getting away from the fact she was a girl and therefore met my parents' criteria!

As my friends arrived, each of them gave me a birthday card and usually a small present such as a toy car or a water pistol – nothing special as for most of my friends money was in short supply in those days. I placed the cards on the mantelpiece with my family cards and then we all sat down around our dining-room table in the big room. There was a lot of chattering and great excitement as we waited for Mum to say we could start. The food at the party was nothing fancy and mainly consisted of jam and fish paste sandwiches, crisps and jelly and ice cream, with some bottles of Tizer bought from over the road. But to us it was a slap-up meal.

Once the food had all been consumed – and there was never any left as we all tucked in enthusiastically – Mum brought out the birthday cake, normally a chocolate sponge she'd made herself, with the appropriate number of candles on. Everyone sang 'Happy Birthday', then I took a deep breath and blew out the candles, while at the same time making a wish, which was usually nothing more profound or earth-shattering than something to the effect that Gloucestershire (the cricket team I supported) would win the County Championship that year. Sadly, that particular wish never came true. The cake was then whisked away and cut into the appropriate number of pieces and put in some tissue paper ready for everyone to take home. We never ate it at the party itself.

Once the food had gone, we played some party games such as musical chairs, pin the tail on the donkey or squeak, piggy, squeak. After these organised games, we were let loose on the field to play for a while on our own; usually we chose football, though sometimes we would see who could climb the highest up one of the trees. Painful as it is to admit it, the winner of this game was normally Judith. You see, I told you she was an honorary boy!

And then it was time for everyone to go home. They all picked up their goody bag containing a piece of birthday cake, some sweets and maybe a little toy (Mum's job at the toy factory came in very handy for this). After they'd all gone, it was just about time for Dad to get home from work and once he'd had his dinner I would get my parents' presents. This varied from year to year but there was always at least one book, usually Dr Dolittle, Worzel Gummidge or Jennings. I always treasured these as they were now my own and I didn't have to give them back to the library and could read them over and over again.

Quite often I would also get a new board game and some Meccano. One year I was given an Airfix helicopter kit, but I'm afraid making models is not my forte and it wasn't a great success. (A failing that has stayed with me for the whole of my life as anyone who has ever seen me try to put together flat-pack furniture will agree wholeheartedly.)

And then it was time for bed after a very happy day.

CHAPTER EIGHT

KNOCK KNEES, LAUGHING GAS AND NITS

Before the days of MMR, triple vaccines and the like, all children were prone to getting the normal childhood diseases. In fact, I seem to remember we were encouraged to get them (somehow) when we were young as this gave you immunity for life. Many of them could cause disastrous complications in later life, especially German measles for pregnant women and mumps for reasons young men will understand!

I have no memory at all of getting measles or whooping cough, though I understand I had both when I was a toddler. Apparently, I had a very mild case of whooping cough as Mum told me later that I just had one whoop and then it was all over.

I can just about remember having scarlet fever as I can still picture the dark room I had to be kept in. Even though it was my own bedroom, having the curtains drawn and the lights permanently off made it seem very scary. However, this was reckoned to be good for the patient as any light was thought to be able to make you go permanently blind when in the throes of this particular disease.

I was also vaguely uneasy about the idea that, having a disease with the word fever in it, I might have to be confined to the Fever Hospital, which was down at the other end of Chatsworth Road. It was a stark forbidding building that looked just like a prison from the outside and was certainly a place no child would ever wish to enter. If we walked down that way, we would go to great lengths to avoid going near it, as we feared we might catch some dreadful disease. I still shudder when I think of it, even today.

In fact, I might have come closer to entering the Fever Hospital than I thought as it did treat cases of scarlet fever. It was opened in December 1870 and housed six typhus wards, two scarlet fever wards, two wards for patients with enteric and two wards for any special cases, catering in all for two hundred patients. In 1871, a specialist smallpox hospital opened next door, made up of four blocks each with eight wards of twelve beds. In the first three days, sixty patients were admitted and by the next month the hospital was filled to capacity. The overflow went to the Fever Hospital, which was increased in size to hold 600 beds. The two hospitals merged in 1921 and became the Eastern Fever Hospital, treating mainly scarlet fever and diphtheria in children, so I could, indeed, have been sent there, if I'd had a more serious case of scarlet fever. It was a lucky escape.

The other two common childhood diseases, mumps and

German measles, came a bit later in my childhood, so I remember them quite well. Of the two, mumps was the worst because it gave me a terrible sore throat and I was unable to eat solid food. Again I was confined to bed for several days, which seemed to be the cure for everything. As it was clearing up, Mum gave me some thick vegetable soup. The soup was okay, but I couldn't eat any of the pieces of vegetable. I shared my bedroom with John, as he must have been on holiday from school at that time. Fortunately for him, he had already had mumps when he was younger so wasn't in any danger of catching it from me. He saw me getting very frustrated as I tried to eat the soup.

He said, 'Are you getting angry because you can't eat the vegetables?'

'No, I'm angry because Mum gave it to me!' I replied.

I'm sure she was only doing what she thought best, though.

German measles was the mildest of all. In fact, I didn't even know I was ill until Mum got the doctor out to look at the rash on my neck and face. He diagnosed German measles and, of course, confinement to bed for two weeks. Throughout the whole two weeks, I didn't actually feel ill at all. Still, it was two weeks off school, so I didn't complain.

The other good thing about being confined to bed was that Dad would set up the television in my bedroom so I could watch it, though, of course, for much of the 1950s, there wasn't a lot on during the day. But I was able to watch *Children's Hour* and then the early evening programmes until it was time for sleep. I guess my parents had to go without their night-time viewing, though this thought never occurred to me at the time.

Fortunately, by the 1950s, some of the more serious and even killer childhood diseases had been conquered by vaccination. Two of the worst had been diphtheria and polio. Although the diphtheria vaccine had been around for some time, it was only in 1955 that Jonas Salk launched his polio vaccine on the world, so I was one of the first to be vaccinated against this dreadful disease. It had no known cure and, if it didn't kill, it could leave children with severely withered limbs. Although it wasn't a common sight, it still wasn't unusual to see children forced to rely on crutches to support their wasted leg muscles. I can remember queuing up at school to receive my diphtheria and polio jabs in a kind of vaccination production line.

As well as the childhood diseases, there were also the usual colds and flu. On one occasion I can remember us all, Mum, Dad and me, laid up with flu at the same time. I don't know how long we were in bed together but it was at least a day, maybe two. On the morning we all began to feel a bit better, Dad got up and said, 'I'm hungry. How about something to eat?' Mum and I agreed with this sentiment, so a few minutes later Dad brought in three plates of beans on toast, which we all devoured eagerly in bed and then got up and continued with our lives.

I also fell prey to the 1957–58 flu epidemic. Known as 'Asian flu' because it was said to have originated in China, this was the most virulent flu outbreak since the 1918 epidemic. The highest rates were among schoolchildren and well over 50 per cent of all young children were affected. When our school succumbed, I was actually one of the last to become a victim and by the time I did get it there was only a handful of pupils left in my class. Although it was fairly mild, two girls from the nearby Girls Secondary Modern School died from the disease and I told my parents about this. Dad told me it was because they didn't stay in bed but went out playing. I was quite satisfied by this explanation and ceased to worry about my fate.

It was while I was laid up in bed that the Munich air disaster happened. Dad had fixed up our television in my bedroom as usual. On the day of the disaster, 6 February 1958, he came home from work at his normal time and came straight in to see me. His first words were: 'How's the big fellow?' I didn't know what he was talking about as I hadn't been watching the television and then he explained to me about the plane crash that had killed and seriously injured a number of the Manchester United football team. By 'the big fellow' he meant Duncan Edwards, generally recognised as one of England's best ever footballers, who was critically ill. We immediately put on the television and saw the news unfold. Sadly, Edwards died a few days later. It was a very distressing time for all football fans, not just Manchester United fans.

As well as taking it easy in bed, colds often necessitated the administration of Vick VapoRub on my chest and sometimes Vick Inhalant, which meant sitting over a bowl of hot water and Vick with a towel over my head, breathing in the health-giving fumes. Both of these were decongestants, which helped ease the symptoms.

I mentioned earlier that the doctor came out to see me when I had German measles and in those days it was quite normal and common to call out the doctor to see you. It was an expected part of the G.P.'s job to be on call twenty-four hours a day, seven days a week. They were called out especially when babies and children were ill. With most people not having their own transport, it was more difficult to get to the doctor's surgery than it is today, so the twenty-four-hour service was much used.

That's not to say that for minor problems and general complaints we didn't go to the surgery because, of course, we did. There were two local practices: one in Chatsworth Road, the other in Brooksby's Walk. We signed on with Dr Price, the furthest away of the two, because we were given to understand he was very good with children. He was an old-school doctor, in his fifties, I should guess, when I first got to know him. He had a younger assistant, Dr Klein, who seemed more go-ahead and more up-to-date in his thinking, but most people seemed to trust Dr Price more.

When you went to the doctor, there was no such thing as making an appointment, you just turned up and queued. The waiting room was set out with chairs all round the wall and a block of something like twenty-five chairs in the centre. You started at the back right chair (nearest to the front door) and worked your way down the centre block.

When you got to the last seat, you then moved on to the front right and worked your way round the wall until eventually you came to the front left, which meant it was your turn next. A bell would signify that you should go in to see Dr Price on the ground floor and a buzzer meant going upstairs to Dr Klein. Often people would pass on hearing the buzzer, preferring to wait for Dr Price. We always did.

I visited the doctor's on a number of occasions and it was

nearly always full, which meant a very long wait. The main reason for my many visits was the wax in my ears. On most occasions Dr Price would tell Dad (it was nearly always Dad I went with) to use an ear dropper to put warm olive oil into my ears every day for a fortnight to soften the wax up and then come back and he would syringe them. Because this was what he always said, Dad once took it on himself to start a two-week regime of putting olive oil into my ears so that when we went to see Dr Price he could dispense with this part of the programme and go straight to the syringing.

Thinking it would be helpful to Dr Price and to the other patients if we went in last, we got there not long before closing time and let the few people that came after us go in front. When we finally got to see Dr Price, Dad told him what we'd done and asked him to syringe my ears.

Dr Price's reply was not what Dad wanted to hear: 'I'm too tired to do it now, I've had a long day. Come back tomorrow.'

But Dad wasn't having any of this. He said, '*You're* feeling tired! Well, so am I. I've been at work all day and we've waited specially while everyone else has been seen to do you a favour and now you tell us to come back tomorrow. My boy needs his ears syringing. He's had the olive oil for two weeks and we're not leaving till you've done it!'

In the face of this onslaught, Dr Price had no alternative but to give in and syringe my ears.

My constant battle against wax culminated in a visit to the Ear, Nose and Throat Hospital on Gray's Inn Road in London. They stuck some long needles down my ears and scraped hard wax off the sides. After I'd had this done, I could hear amazingly well for a few weeks and then the wax returned again. It was a losing battle!

I also visited the Children's Hospital in Hackney several times as Mum thought I was knock-kneed and wanted me to walk straight. All I can remember about those visits is walking up and down the floor of the room in a straight line; I don't remember anyone actually doing anything physical to straighten my legs out.

The only other childhood problem I had was eczema on the back of my right hand. For this I had to visit the Metropolitan Hospital in Dalston, where I had cream applied to my hand until the eczema eventually disappeared.

There were a lot of hospitals around then. As well as the Hackney Hospital, the Fever Hospital, the Children's Hospital and the Metropolitan Hospital, there was also the German Hospital in Dalston Road. I never knew why anyone would call a hospital the German Hospital, as of course in the 1950s Germany and Germans were still country and persona non grata. Why they had this special privilege was hard for my young mind to fathom. I subsequently discovered that, when the hospital was first opened in 1845, it catered for the German immigrant population, which, at that time, was the largest immigrant community in the country, numbering some 30,000. Many of them lived and worked in very poor conditions in the East End and this, combined with poverty and the inability to speak English properly, left them unable to use the medical resources available so a German pastor and a doctor made it their mission to build a hospital to meet the needs of their community. Not one of those hospitals is still open today, most of the services having been transferred to the new Homerton University Hospital, opened in 1986.

When a prescription needed to be filled, my parents mostly collected it from Benjy's in Chatsworth Road. Sometimes, when the prescription resulted from an out-of-hours doctor's visit, Dad went by bus to the all-night chemist near Hackney Downs Station, a good fifteen-minute bus ride away. If it was a very out-of-hours visit, he would have to get the night bus.

Apart from the time we all had 'flu, I don't remember Mum and Dad being ill except on one occasion when Dad had to go into hospital to have an operation to remove a varicose vein in his leg. In those days, children were not allowed on to the wards even to see their parents so I didn't see him for over a week. It was the longest I had ever gone without seeing him, so I found it a very difficult time.

Both before and after his hospital sojourn, Dad was laid up at home for a while, having to rest his leg. He couldn't work, especially as the nature of his job meant standing up all day bashing a mallet and chisel into wood. Because he was self-employed, he didn't pay the full National Insurance stamp so it meant he wasn't entitled to full National Assistance, as it was known then, and we had to get by on a greatly reduced level of income for a few weeks. Of course, I didn't really understand any of this but our position was brought home to me one day when I was out shopping with Mum and I saw a small toy soldier I wanted. Normally, if I asked for something like that, she would buy it for me, but this time she said she didn't have enough money. I didn't really understand this refusal and was most disappointed but I did realise it had something to do with

Dad not being at work. Truth be told, I expect Mum was even more upset than me at having to disappoint me.

Although I never saw Mum ill, I realised in later life that she suffered from the most terrible migraines. And I mean migraines, not just bad headaches, but the real thing with flashing lights, dizzy spells, light sensitivity and all the rest. Somehow she still managed to look after me during those bouts, which could last up to a day. It wouldn't have occurred to her not to soldier on.

Going to see the doctor was one thing, but visiting the dentist was another thing altogether. Judging by the number of times my friends and I had to have fillings or extractions, I can only assume dentists were paid by the number of teeth they filled or took out. Given that in general we ate a lot better in the 1950s, there must be some explanation – perhaps we had lots of sweets with our healthy diet.

Our dentist was Mr Thomas, who had his surgery in a very picturesque setting in front of St Augustine's Tower at the end of the Narroway in Mare Street. My memory of those visits is going into a very dark and gloomy waiting room in keeping with the nature of the fate about to befall me. After waiting for a while, I would be ushered upstairs and sat in the large black chair, where wadding would be stuffed into my mouth and a black (why was everything black in the dentist?) mask strapped over my mouth and nose. Laughing gas was then pumped into me to put me to sleep. The name 'laughing gas' was a misnomer if ever there was one. It was no laughing matter, I can tell you! The next thing I knew was waking up with a numb feeling in my mouth and blood still dribbling out. The nurse would always helpfully suggest that Mum buy me an ice cream to stop the bleeding and make me feel better. This was all well and good but my mouth was so numb that I couldn't eat it, or anything else come to that, for some time after, by which time the bleeding had long since ceased of its own accord.

The waiting room at the dentist was different to the doctor's in that you didn't have to move round – you just stayed in your seat until you were called. However, on one occasion, to take my mind off the impending doom, I decided that I would move round so that every time someone got up to see the dentist I would move into their seat. After doing so a couple of times, a new patient arrived and sat in the seat I had originally sat in. This wasn't part of the game at all and I was absolutely distraught that someone had sat in 'my' seat. I burst into floods of tears until Mum explained to the person concerned why I was crying and she very kindly moved.

I also visited another dentist on occasion, actually closer to where we lived in Goulton Road, just off Lower Clapton Road. This was an NHS clinic and was where we were referred if necessary after one of the regular medical checks we received at school. At that time, we had regular visits from a doctor, a dentist and, of course, the dreaded nit nurse, universally known as 'Nitty Nora', who used to run her special comb soaked in antiseptic through your hair to see if you had nits. Fortunately, I never did and therefore never needed any treatment for the condition. However, the same could not be said for the dentist as, in spite of seemingly having every tooth either extracted or filled by Mr Thomas, the school dentist sometimes found that I was in dire need of yet another extraction or filling. When that was the case, I was taken to the Goulton Road Clinic for the work to be done. I think this only happened on a couple of occasions but, as bad as Mr Thomas's surgery was, this one was even worse! The main reason was that there was no full anaesthetic, just a cocaine injection to numb the area. On those occasions, I was fully conscious and highly aware of the dentist pulling and tugging at the offending tooth. I can still remember to this day with a shudder of horror the feeling of the tooth being crushed rather than pulled cleanly.

Sometimes a loose tooth fell out naturally, or after help from my parents. My best remembered occasion of such help was when Grandpa rolled up his copy of the *Daily Mirror* and said, 'Open your mouth,' and then took a jab at my loose tooth. I just flinched back so he never actually touched it. Shortly afterwards, it fell out of its own accord – perhaps in shock.

Of course, when a loose tooth came out, it was left under the pillow at night to await the arrival of the tooth fairy with her sixpenny piece. I'm glad to say she never once failed me.

CHAPTER NINE

CROSS-COUNTRY RUNNING AND GANGS

'There's a letter for you from Parmiter's,' Mum said, bringing the morning post in about a week after my last day at Rushmore.

I grabbed it and hurriedly tore it open. 'It's my joining instructions,' I said excitedly.

My first day was to be Tuesday, 9 September but before that I had to get myself kitted out with the school uniform. Unlike Rushmore, wearing school uniform was compulsory and there was only one supplier, Henry Taylor and Sons of Hoe Street, Walthamstow. So one day during the summer holidays, off I went with Mum to get myself sorted out with blazer, trousers, socks, tie and cap, as well as P.E. and sports kit.

Like Rushmore, there were four houses, but this time they were named after former school benefactors. I was to be in

Carter House, whose colour was yellow. There was also Mayhew (white), Lee (green) and Renvoize (blue). I was later given to understand that the reason why there was no red team dated back to the War, when red dye was in short supply and Mayhew was changed to white. During the holiday, I also bought a geometry set and a new satchel ready for the big day.

And so on Tuesday, 9 September, I got up bright and early, put on my brand-new uniform, Brylcreemed my hair and waited for Bob Marriott to call, as we had agreed.

'You look very smart,' Mum said.

I smiled and felt quite proud but before I could reply there was a knock on the door.

'How are you feeling?' Bob asked as I opened it.

'A bit nervous,' I confessed.

Bob nodded. 'Me too.'

Although we were both apprehensive about what lay in store for us as we made our way to the bus stop in Lower Clapton Road to catch either the 557 or the 653 trolleybus to school, we nevertheless felt very grown up, going off on our own on the bus to grammar school: we weren't juniors any more, we were big boys. What a shock when we reached the school, though! We went into the playground and there were boys there anything up to six feet tall with whiskers and very deep voices and suddenly we felt really small again. How we longed to be safely back in our Junior School, where we ourselves had been the big boys. We really hadn't expected this at all. It came as a big shock but at least we weren't alone. We could see huddled in one corner of the playground a group of small boys obviously feeling as inferior as we did, so we went over and joined them. I think there was a feeling of safety in numbers.

When the bell went to summon us for our first lesson, we had to line up in the classes given us in the joining letter. Several teachers emerged from the school building, all wearing their university gowns, to greet the first years. Our teacher led us off up the stairs to our classroom. Mr Blake was our form teacher. He had a strange gait, leaning forward as he walked. We learnt later that this was due to an unfortunate wartime injury, or as one of the older boys at the school, Chris Turner, so delicately put it when he overhead some of us talking about it in the playground, 'Blakey? The way 'e walks. Oh yeah, only 'ad a bayonet shoved up his fuckin' arse by the bleedin' Jerries, didn't he!' We all shuddered – it sounded like an excruciatingly painful experience.

When we'd all settled down in the classroom, Mr Blake gave us an introduction to life at Parmiter's. He was very pleasant and reassuring and we thought that perhaps things wouldn't be too bad after all. Sadly, that impression was soon to be completely shattered.

When he finished, he went off to teach another class because, unlike Junior School, we had a different teacher for each subject. As he left, another teacher swept in through the door like a Force 8 gale, his gown billowing out behind him. When he reached the front of the class, he proceeded to harangue us all in French. Oh dear, this was something completely alien to us! It was obvious we had done something wrong but no one knew what it could be. Mr Moore might have had his off-days but I'd far rather the comfort and security of his class than this any day.

Eventually, this human tornado calmed down and explained to us that we had to stand up whenever a teacher came into the room. Of course, he knew that we wouldn't have known this and his angry outburst was all done for effect but I never trusted Mr Engledow from that day until I left school, eight years later.

The rest of that first day passed in something of a blur as we were taken from classroom to classroom and introduced to a number of teachers and many new subjects. At lunchtime, we all made our way down to the dining room to sample school dinners. Sadly, they were no better than those experienced at Rushmore and, indeed, consisted of much the same 'muck', as we liked to call it. That first day, it was the familiar mushy mince. It looked so unappetising that I really couldn't face eating it and just pushed it around my plate, mixing it up with the mashed potato. Roger Gooding, the boy sitting next to me, took one look at the mess I'd created and said, 'That looks like a plate of diarrhoea.'

Well, if I didn't fancy it before, I certainly didn't now, so I just pushed it to one side. And it didn't get any better; for afters we had semolina. Yuck!

What was different about this dining hall, though, was the sheer size of it and the number of boys staying to dinner. At Rushmore, there were only about thirty or forty, certainly no more than fifty. Here, practically the whole school of several hundred stayed to school dinners. Hardly anyone went home as most homes were too far away for a lunchtime return. There was an option to take sandwiches but most parents saw school dinners as a chance to get some wholesome hot food inside their children.

Also different was the fact that the teachers joined us for dinner. They sat together on the 'top table', apart from the teacher on duty, who prowled round the dining hall to make sure we weren't misbehaving. As if we would! Well, at least only when his back was turned. Flicking mash at the boys on the next table with a spoon was always good for a laugh and this would result in a full-scale food fight while the teacher was not looking. Occasionally, someone would be caught at it and ordered out of his seat to stand in full view of everyone in the corner of the room for the rest of dinnertime. Depending on the teacher, he might receive some extra punishment in the form of lines or detention, or even a smack round the head.

Some teachers were harder than others and we quickly learnt who we could chance our arm with and who we couldn't. Of course, corporal punishment was still part and parcel of a teacher's armoury at this time and could range from just a quick clip round the ear, through a sharp tap with a ruler across the knuckles, a smack across the legs or bottom to a formal caning by the Headmaster, with your name written in the punishment book and your crime recorded for all time. Fortunately, although I suffered a few whacks of various kinds during my years at Parmiter's, I am not recorded in the punishment book.

At the end of the day, somewhat dazed, bewildered and confused, Bob and I made our way to the bus stop to catch the trolleybus back home. Naturally, along with a number of other boys, we went upstairs so we could get a good view and play around out of sight of the conductor. The drawback with upstairs was that in those days smoking was allowed on the upper deck of London buses, so there was generally a bit of a blue haze and a smell of tobacco smoke, accompanied by much spluttering and coughing. The pungent aroma of smoke was somewhat ameliorated along Cambridge Heath Road by the very pleasant scent that emanated from a perfume factory close by. Strangely, we only ever smelled it in the afternoons; I can't remember ever smelling it in the morning. But once into Mare Street it was back to tobacco. Still we felt it was worth it to be out of the conductor's gaze. Every now and then, he would venture up to cry out, 'Any more fares, please?' but we could always hear him coming up the stairs, so it gave us plenty of time to sit down like little angels before resuming whatever it was we were doing as soon as we heard his footsteps going back down.

On arrival home, Mum said, 'How was your first day, then?'

I replied simply, 'I'm not sure,' before adding, 'but I will go back again tomorrow.' Not that I had a choice but it sounded brave.

In fact, it had all been overwhelming. Meeting new classmates, being overawed by much older boys, new teachers, a new geography in a much bigger school to get to know my way round, the fact we were all called by our surname instead of our Christian name, the bus journeys. It was all so different to the cosy familiar little world of Rushmore but I said I would go back again the next day and back I went.

Gradually, however, things began to fall into place. I made some new friends, particularly Murray Glickman and John Hill. I sat next to Murray in our own form classroom. He was a Jewish lad so to some extent I related easily to him. I also discovered after a week or so that he actually knew how to play clobby. Amazing! One thing I didn't quite understand, however, was that, whereas I went into the normal morning assembly with all the other boys, Murray attended a special one for Jewish boys, of whom there were only about a dozen or so in the whole school. This didn't bother me too much, but when he took some days off for what he called Jewish holidays with strange-sounding names like Rosh Hashanah and Yom Kippur I needed some answers as I thought surely I must be entitled to these too.

So, one night I said to Dad, 'My friend Murray is off school tomorrow for a Jewish holiday. Shouldn't I be on holiday as well?'

He laughed and said, 'You can't have Jewish holidays because you're not Jewish.'

Dad explained that this was because Jewish descent is through the mother, and Mum was actually brought up as a Catholic. He went on to say that, although he and his family upheld some Jewish traditions, they were not in the main religious and that he personally didn't believe in God anyway. But he said that he wouldn't force his views on me and that when I was old enough I should make up my own mind. As far as he was concerned, I started with a blank canvas and I could become anything I wanted – Jewish, Christian, atheist, it was entirely up to me. I have always been grateful for this and for the fact that nothing was forced on me at an early age. However, at the time I was a bit disappointed that I couldn't have a couple of days off for Rosh Hashanah, like Murray.

John Hill resembled my friend Andy, in that he was a bit corpulent and loved all sport, so we hit it off there straight away.

As time went on, we were to become very good friends, later sharing many interests, including Gilbert and Sullivan and folk music as well as sport.

Meeting lots of new teachers was a completely different experience and they came in all shapes and sizes, with their own individual and sometimes eccentric personalities. The only subject our form master, Mr Blake, took us for was Maths. English was taught by Mr Deeble, who rejoiced in the nickname 'Daphne'. He was a decent enough sort, not taken to doling out corporal punishment. What Murray, John and I really liked about him was that once a month or so he would suspend the English lesson and hold a general knowledge quiz. As he came into the room, he would say, 'Quiz positions,' and we all had to move round as the way he organised the quiz was to ask the first question of the boy in the back left-hand corner and work his way down until someone could answer the question correctly. That boy would then move to the back left, while everyone else moved down a place. This continued with boys moving up and down, according to your answer. By the end of a lesson, Murray, John and I would invariably hold the top three places – although sometimes Pete Smith managed to sneak in! So, when Mr Deeble came in and said, 'Quiz positions,' we had to assume the place we were in at the end of the last quiz. On one occasion, he said he was going to start at the other end so that we were actually in the bottom three positions. Everyone else in the class thought this was very funny and had a good laugh at our expense. By the end of the lesson, we were the top three again.

Of course, French was taken by Mr Engledow – the teacher

who had shouted at us in French on the first day. I never did like him and he could be very cutting and sarcastic at times. I was reasonably good at French and eventually took it at A-level, but I never looked forward to his lessons. Though here again, about once or twice a term, he would suspend the lesson and tell us a story about an English family travelling to France, trying to teach us something about the geography and customs of the country. Those fairly rare breaks from language lessons were very welcome.

Mr Simms, our History teacher, was a great character. He had actually written the textbooks we used throughout our first four years up to O-level standard. Between September and May, he was rarely in on a Monday morning as he was a Chelsea F.C. shareholder and would either have spent the weekend celebrating or drowning his sorrows. I think the only times he came in was when Chelsea drew! He was also a great follower of the gee-gees and there was one memorable occasion when he was describing the Battle of Agincourt to us. He was explaining how the French cavalry charged at the English archers and said, 'So the horses were all lined up, waiting for the signal to charge... which reminds me, I haven't put my bet on today.' At which point he opened up his briefcase, took out a copy of the *Racing Post* and said, 'Open your books to page one hundred and read up about it.' He then slouched back in his chair, with his feet up on the table, looking through his paper. In spite of this somewhat wayward behaviour, he was an excellent teacher and really brought history alive.

Geography was taught by Mr Hume. I say taught, but really he did very little teaching; he was dire. He came into the class every lesson with his blue attaché case from which he proceeded to take out reams of duplicated notes and distribute them round the class. Our job was to read the papers and try to commit what was written to memory while he sat at his desk, marking papers from other classes.

Science was never really my forte, though I was vaguely interested in biology. Along with physics, this was taken by Mr Martin, whose nickname was 'Genie'. No one knew why, it just seemed to be a school tradition that went back many years. Having said that science was not my thing, it was quite exciting at first to go into a proper science lab and see all the test tubes, scales, Florence flasks, evaporating dishes and the rest – objects most of us had never come across before. But most exciting were the Bunsen burners, which you could use for boring experiments or they could be put to much better use, when the teacher wasn't looking, by pointing one at a fellow pupil and having a Bunsen burner fight.

For some obscure reason best known to himself, our chemistry teacher, Mr Thrasher, didn't approve of this behaviour and, in his own words, 'would come down like a ton of bricks' on anyone caught doing it. Mr Thrasher's nickname was 'Noddy' as he was always nodding his head. He also had a bit of a speech impediment, which meant he sprayed out a stream of spit whenever he used the letter 's'. As far as I was concerned, though, the excitement soon palled when we had to perform experiments like seeing whether the litmus paper turned red or blue and so on. I much preferred Mr Simms and his cavalry charges or Daphne's quizzes.

Our music teacher was Mr Taylor. Sadly, he never actually

seemed very interested in the subject and it was all just a repeat of learning to sing the folk songs we had already learnt at Rushmore. Fortunately, however, we did have one teacher, a Welshman called Mr Leonard, whom we nicknamed 'Curly' because he was completely bald. Even though his actual job was teaching Maths, he had a real passion for music. He decided to make it his mission to create a choir worthy of the best school choirs in the country and held auditions after school. Although I had been one of Mr Brown's 'growlers', I nevertheless decided to go along and see if I could get into the choir. Mr Leonard's opinion of my voice was completely different and he gave me a place straight away.

We used to meet once a week at the end of a school day and, when rehearsing for a special event, on Saturday mornings as well. Mr Leonard taught us much more interesting songs and quite complicated choral pieces. Until he came along, the school choir consisted solely of boys whose voices hadn't yet broken and their function was mainly to sing at morning assembly. The choir also sang on a couple of special occasions: Speech Day, when the end-of-year prizes were given out, and the Christmas Carol concert. But Curly kept boys on into their tenor, baritone and bass years and taught us how to sing harmonies and much more difficult pieces. The most demanding piece we ever learnt was 'Sleepers Awake', a Bach cantata, written in four-part harmony – a bit different from Tennyson's 'The Owl'! Mr Leonard was finally given the accolade of seeing us, his choir, out of all the schools in London being chosen to sing on the stage of the Royal Festival Hall at a special Christmas Carol concert.

Physical Training and Games were taken by Mr Hollyhock,

probably the most unfit teacher in the school. Often he would set us off doing some exercise in the school hall (which doubled as the gym, with wall bars and vaulting horses, etc.) while he went outside for a fag. He was also a noted visitor to The Approach, the pub across the road from the school, at lunchtimes and after work. While in the hall, he would bark out orders – 'Running on the spot, begin!' and so on. He never actually taught any techniques of how to do anything but expected us to be able to vault over a horse, climb the wall bars or do somersaults just because we were boys, I suppose, and we should know that sort of thing. One thing he wouldn't stand was backchat. If he gave an order, he expected it to be obeyed without question. If he saw two boys talking, his favourite rejoinder was to say, 'What was that little remark?' It was a catchphrase of his that was used throughout the school and indeed is still fondly remembered to this day by Old Parmiterians.

For Games, we used to have to take a special coach to our school sportsground, which was situated in Higham's Park, just at the back of Walthamstow Greyhound Stadium. This was a big area comprising about four or five football pitches on it, with, during our first year, a dreadfully decrepit changing room that looked as though it had been thrown up in a couple of hours sometime in the 1890s. There were no proper wash facilities and certainly no showers or baths. During the summer holidays at the end of our first year, new brick changing rooms were built with communal showers. Most boys took the showers in their stride but, for some, at the age of twelve and just entering puberty, there was certainly some embarrassment and a reluctance to enter the showers with other boys with no clothes on. At first, some tried to go in with their shorts still on, but Mr Hollyhock wouldn't have any of that nonsense and made them take them off. I suppose for many of us it was the first time that the question of sexuality reared its head, something which, of course, was to happen a lot more as we came into our early and mid-teens.

Once we'd got dressed, we went into a small canteen, where we could buy either orange squash or lime juice plus a biscuit – Wagon Wheels were the favourite. I always had lime juice but nearly everyone else had orange squash. I could never understand this because a) lime juice tasted so much better to me and b) we could get orange squash any time we liked, being the staple drink in most homes. After that, it was time to get the bus back to school. Depending on the driver and the mood of Mr Hollyhock, you could get dropped off near home if you asked nicely.

The Games afternoons were arranged on a whole-year basis rather than just one class, so several matches took place – either football or cricket depending on the season. Because of this, other teachers came along, mostly the younger ones, and, although they might be Maths, Science or English teachers, they all looked much fitter than Mr Hollyhock. As with gym, there was never any instruction or coaching, we just had to get on with it. The only break in the football or cricket routine came when the school sports were held or when we had to go cross-country running.

The week before the school sports were held, each house had its qualifying events to see who would represent them in the finals. As at Junior School, I was usually one of Carter's two representatives in the sprint, now extended to 100 yards, but again never actually managed to win (I think second place was my best). In the second year, I discovered a talent for the triple jump; although there was a certain amount of technique required, the event did favour the faster runners to get speed up on the runway before the jump. This was an event I did win several times over the years and eventually went on to represent the school in inter-school matches and championships.

Cross-country running was always held in the worst months of winter. We had to run up the road from the school ground across the level crossing at Higham's Park Station and then into Epping Forest, squelching through the mud and decayed leaves in the pouring rain, or, worse still, sometimes in a snow blizzard, before returning along the roads. It was torture of the highest order and sometimes made you think that it might be better just to refuse to go and face detention or six of the best. Teachers would sometimes be stationed along the way to make sure you ran the course, though more often than not they didn't bother, especially if it was raining. Mr Hollyhock in particular preferred his fag in the warmth of the pavilion.

The other two subjects it was my misfortune to have to take part in were art and woodwork. Woodwork was carried out in a special workshop in another school, Mowlem Street School, about a ten-minute walk away from Parmiter's. Now you would have thought that with my father being a woodcarver by trade I might have made a good fist at woodworking, but as it happened I was completely hopeless. The first thing we ever made was a pencil sharpener. All this consisted of was a piece of sandpaper stuck to a wooden block, on which you rubbed your pencil up and down to sharpen it. I just about managed this but the items we had to make afterwards got progressively harder. The following week, there was a toothbrush rack, then a pencil box and a ship!

As the projects got more difficult, my efforts looked less and less like the object they were supposed to be until my teacher, Mr Gibson, just gave up and didn't really bother any more. After giving me some wood, a plane, a hammer, some nails and some glue, he told me to do what I liked. Fortunately, Murray was as good as I was, so we spent the lesson playing around with the wood and chatting. Mention of the glue reminds me that this was probably the most interesting part of woodwork classes as Mr Gibson used to boil up some concoction – 'horse glue' he called it – in a big pot, which he decanted into smaller pots to dole out to everyone. The pot boiled away throughout the lesson emitting a very powerful, though I have to say not unpleasant odour.

As for art, I still hadn't progressed much beyond the stage of a circle for the head, a bigger one for the body and limbs sticking out at forty-five-degree angles. Mr Williams, the art teacher, also despaired and gave up teaching me at an early stage. I just wasn't very good with my hands.

As well as staying behind once a week for the choir, I became interested in another after-school club – the archaeology club, run by Mr Gibson. I found this really intriguing as it continued my interest in history in a very practical way. As well as meeting after school, we would sometimes go out at the weekends, either to visit a museum, especially the London Museum, or even to look round old archaeological sites such as Ambresbury

Banks, an Iron Age settlement near Epping, an Iron Age fort near Loughton and a Mesolithic site at High Beech. On this last visit, Mr Gibson told us to bring trowels so we could have a dig round. It was here that I found a Stone Age scraper. I took it home and put it into the cupboard in the big room. A few days later, it was missing so I asked Mum and Dad if they'd seen it. Mum said she'd thrown it away because she thought it was just an old stone from the garden. Aaaarrrgggghhh!

We also visited the big Roman site at St Albans, where I bought some Roman artefacts from the souvenir shop. This time I made sure I explained to Mum and Dad what those rusty old nails and bits of bone were.

The late 1950s and early 1960s was an exciting time in archaeology as it was in 1959 that the husband and wife team of Mary and Louis Leakey discovered the remains of what became known initially as 'Zinjanthropus Man' in Olduvai Gorge, East Africa. The specimen's age of 1.75 million years radically altered the accepted ideas about the timescale of human evolution. Mr Gibson made sure we were kept up to date with all the latest developments. I was absolutely fascinated by news of these discoveries and it became my ambition to one day visit Olduvai Gorge, something I eventually managed almost fifty years later, in 2006.

Finally, of course, there was the Headmaster, Mr A. Hopkins. He never taught any classes but stayed in his office all day, every day apart from taking morning assembly. The reason he hardly ever came out of his office was well known to the whole school. It was because he bore an uncanny resemblance to Adolf Hitler, even down to the small moustache. We were sure he must be in hiding and that's why he never came out. The clinching piece of evidence was his initials.

Parmiter's had a large playground but, unlike Junior School, we only had playtime in the morning, though it was now called 'break'. As most pupils stayed to dinner, it was much more used in the middle of the day than Rushmore's had been and at first we continued to play the same sort of games. There were the seasonal games like conkers and marbles, plus football and cricket. Although War and Cowboys and Indians dropped out of the picture very soon, we did manage to find other ways of having mock fighting games, especially when Robert Kitchen, who was nicknamed 'Feg', formed his gang. I can't remember the origins of this now, but the Feg Gang was opposed by me and my friends, and, in the early days we used to run around firing our pretend guns and so on. The older boys never joined in this sort of thing and for us it also gradually petered out as we grew up.

There was a much quieter air about break time generally and groups of boys would be seen all round the playground just talking in pairs or groups. Some of this discussion was about schoolwork and trying to extract some information about last night's homework before it had to be handed in; a lot of it was about sport; but more and more as we entered our teenage years, it was about girls. Having left them behind at Junior School, many of us had not really had much to do with them other than female relations but there was a growing realisation among all of us that there was more to girls than cissy games and having the odd tomboy over to make up the numbers at birthday parties. There were a few rude jokes and poems but the real breakthrough came when Terry Gregory announced to a group

189

of us one day the sensational news that he had actually touched a girl's breast. He said he had been out with his (female) cousin and some of her friends in Epping Forest and had slipped away with one of the friends for a 'snog'.

'And then,' announced Terry to his stunned audience, 'I put my hand down inside the front of her blouse.'

We listened open-mouthed, itching to hear where this was going to lead.

'Did you actually touch her tits?' asked someone.

Terry grinned. 'What do you think?'

'What were they like, Tel?'

'They were very soft,' he replied.

'Did you get a look?'

'No,' he said, 'she wouldn't let me undo her blouse, so I had to touch her up outside her bra.'

Although we all felt this was a bit of an anti-climax, nevertheless Terry had managed more than any of us had done so he was still someone to be looked up to as the first of our group to have any real sort of sexual experience with a girl.

The first boy to claim that he had actually seen a girl's naked breast was Ronald Dibley, but no one believed him. I think this disbelief really arose from the fact that he was a bit of an outsider to our group and wasn't particularly popular so we thought he was just trying to make himself sound big to ingratiate himself with us but, for all we knew, he may well have been telling the truth. However, this dismissal of his claim didn't stop other boys making various assertions about how far they'd gone until the novelty wore off a bit as we grew up and discussions turned to other matters.

Later on in my time at Parmiter's, the Headmaster ordered that the playground be marked out as a tennis court and a net purchased. This was to allow Graham Stilwell to practise after and even during school time. Graham was in the year above me and became one of Britain's best tennis players, winning the under-18 and under-21 British titles and finishing runner-up at the 1963 junior Australian Championships after losing out to the great John Newcombe. As an adult, for a while he was ranked the number-two British player. Mr Hopkins was very proud of him and, whenever he was playing in a tournament, he would keep the whole school updated on Graham's progress at morning assembly. Graham left school when he was sixteen but that didn't stop the announcements and we all knew what was coming when the Headmaster began his normal morning assembly talk with the words: 'Some of you older boys will remember Graham Stilwell...'

We had another well-known sportsman at the school in my time, boxer Mickey Carter, who represented Great Britain in the 1968 Olympic Games, losing in his third-round tie to the eventual gold medallist, Valerian Sokolov. Not bad going for a school not noted for its sporting prowess.

My own school career progressed fairly steadily. I remained in the A stream but, unlike Rushmore, I was not at the top of it, managing to hold a comfortable middling position in the class. My friend Murray was generally top, along with a few others who were obviously destined for university. The problem for me really was that I didn't get on with science and, as I've said, one subject that I might have been interested in, Geography, was completely ruined by Mr Hume's method of teaching – or non-teaching.

I was quite good at arithmetic and algebra but geometry completely floored me. By the time we got to study for our O-levels, we had a new Maths teacher, Mr Beighton, whom we nicknamed 'Streaky' as a sort of play on Beighton sounding like bacon. After a while, we were told that in his previous school he was known as 'Jif', though no one knew why. Very loud, he was not averse to throwing blackboard rubbers at pupils he felt weren't listening to him. Sometimes he would prowl round the class while we were working and, if he thought you weren't working hard enough or he spotted you talking to your neighbour, he'd quite likely clip you round the ear with a ruler. If you felt hard done by and protested at either of these forms of punishment, his stock answer was: 'Who do you think you are, a sea-lawyer or something?' In spite of his attempts to make us pay attention, I still never managed to get to grips with geometry and I failed my Maths O-level because of it, though I did manage to pass the Oxford University Proficiency in Arithmetic exam with a high mark.

At the end of the fourth form, there was the not-so-little matter of at last being able to dispose of our school caps. Until then we all had to wear them on the way to and from school. In the morning we had to put them on as soon as we left home and in the evening we weren't allowed to take them off before reaching home. Because this rule applied to the first four forms, it meant that most of us were fifteen, and well past the age when we thought we should be wearing school caps on our heads before we were allowed to leave them off outside school.

We all hated it and most boys took the chance that no teacher would see them and took them off once they were on the bus.

If you were seen without your cap, it was instant detention. No appeal, straight in the next day. As we came out of school on our last day at the end of the fourth year, a large number of us threw our caps into the air and cheered. They landed in the road outside. To the applause of the rest of us, someone then lit a match and set fire to them, creating a big bonfire of caps in the middle of the public highway. Naturally, a few of the more daring boys waded into the pile to pick up some burning caps and hurl them around. A blazing-cap fight ensued until some of the teachers came out and put a stop to it. A spectacular end to the hated cap-wearing rule!

Given how my future turned out, it is not surprising that my favourite subjects were English and History, and at the end of my fourth year I gained four O-levels in English Language, English Literature, History and, in spite of, rather than because of, Mr Engledow, French. Part of the O-level exam was an oral test when we had to speak to the examiner and answer questions in French. To prepare us for this, the school engaged a French student, whom we had to see once a week for about half an hour or so. During this session, we were only allowed to speak French. The problem was that she was an extremely attractive girl, only a couple of years older than us, and it was very difficult to concentrate on talking about Mrs Travendamp and her lost umbrella or whatever it was. Whoever thought that appointing a good-looking eighteen- or nineteen-year-old girl to engage with a group of spotty sixteen-year-old adolescent boys in an attempt to help them with their French obviously had no idea what thoughts went through the minds of such youngsters.

I now had to make a decision about whether to continue at

school or leave. Even though my friend John had gained seven O-levels, he decided it was time to get out and earn some money. It sounded quite tempting and I talked it over with Mum and Dad. They said it was up to me what I did but Dad in particular advised me very strongly to stay on as he hoped I would follow my brother John and go to university. His view was that he didn't want me to finish up like him doing hard manual work all my life and that I should continue with my education to ensure this didn't happen, something that was denied to him as he had had to leave school at the age of fourteen to earn money to help support his parents with their large family. After considering my options for a while, I decided to take Dad's advice and stay on. The fact I only had four O-levels meant it was a bit touch and go whether I would be allowed to go straight on to take my A-levels but in the end the school agreed and I chose, not surprisingly, English, History and French. And so I moved on to the sixth form and became one of those six-foot-tall boys with whiskers and a deep voice who had so overawed me on my first day, all those years ago.

Although now we were treated much more like adults and generally had an easier life, I became more and more disinterested in schoolwork. For me there were a lot more interesting things to do. French was still a bit of a problem, thanks to Mr Engledow, whom I thoroughly loathed, and English was good but a bit touch-and-go because one of our set books was *Tom Jones* by Henry Fielding, which I found unutterably boring and difficult to read. As it happened, the film *Tom Jones*, starring Albert Finney, came out while we were studying and was on at the Hackney Pavilion. Another friend of mine, Herb Tyler, was also doing English A-level and so we asked our teacher, Mr Quincey, if we could go and see it one afternoon instead of doing an English Literature lesson. We said it would help if we could visualise it as the book was so difficult but he refused. So, the next day, we went anyway. On our return to school the following day, Joe Quincey (as he was known) asked to see us and wanted to know why we had deliberately disobeyed his order.

'I'm sorry, but we just felt it would help us pass our A-level,' I said.

Somewhat surprisingly, he merely replied, 'Don't be sorry.'

There followed a strained silence as we didn't know how to respond to this. Eventually, Mr Quincey broke it by saying, 'Never say you're sorry. If you do something, stick by it. If you think you are doing something wrong, don't do it in the first place.' After another short silence, he added, 'Did the film help?'

'Yes, I think I have a better understanding of what the book is about now,' I told him.

He told us to go back to our class and that was that.

Although in fact I never really did get to grips with *Tom Jones*, Joe Quincey's little discourse on 'never saying sorry' has stuck with me right until now. While I can't agree that you should never say sorry, I have always taken the point that you shouldn't do something in the first place if you feel you might be sorry for it later.

History was my best subject but even here there was a problem. We were studying for three papers, the first two on Modern British History and Modern Europe, both of which

I felt very comfortable with, but the third paper was on Roman Britain. Our main book for this was *Roman Britain* by Professor Ian Richmond. Early on in the book, describing the position before the Roman conquest, Richmond wrote that the leader of the Catuvellauni tribe, Cunobelinus, held 'virtual suzerainty of south-eastern Britain'. I had no idea what this meant as I had never come across the word suzerainty before and it just made me lose all interest in the Romans. This might sound very silly, looking back on it. I could have guessed what it meant from the context; I could have looked it up in the dictionary; I could have asked Mr Simms, but, because I was rapidly losing interest in school, I couldn't really be bothered even with a subject I enjoyed.

One thing I did like about History was our visits out to various places, though two of these were a bit fraught. The first was when Mr Simms arranged for the History A-level group to visit Parliament. This was due to take place on 21 January 1965. A few days before the due date, it was announced that Sir Winston Churchill was very ill and it was expected that he could die at any time. We were hoping and praying that he would last out till after 21 January for we knew that, as soon as he died, Parliament would be suspended and a period of mourning announced. As it happened, he lived for a few more days, dying on 24 January, so we got to Parliament and saw the House of Commons in action, something I did find very interesting.

When Churchill died, there was lot of discussion among us about his contribution to the War effort. I knew that people of my parents' generation greatly revered Churchill as the man who won the War and that without his foresight, energy, tactical planning and morale-raising speeches we would surely have lost to Hitler. And this went for everyone, even Labour supporters: Dad, for example, who I am certain voted Labour in 1945, nevertheless gave the Conservative Churchill full credit for winning the War. However, the general opinion among my generation when he died was that others could have done the same job – Labour leader Clement Attlee, for example. Although I personally did not agree with this view, I think it proved a significant watershed in the post-war era in lessening the impact made by the War on our everyday life. In the 1950s, it was all-pervasive, but now the generation of political satire and Beatlemania had found its own voice and a new era was dawning, 'forged in the white heat of technology', as our new Prime Minister, the Labour Party's Harold Wilson, put it, that owed nothing to the Second World War.

The other visit was to the Roman Villa at Lullingstone in Kent. Before we went, Herb and I asked if we were covered by insurance in case anything happened to us while out on the trip and we were told we wouldn't be. We decided not to go and instead visited the London Museum on our own. On our arrival at school the next day, Mr Engledow, who was by then our form master, asked where we had been the day before and we told him we'd been to the London Museum. He said that counted as an unauthorised absence and demanded a letter from our parents, telling him where we were.

I had, over the years, given Dad the benefit of my views on Mr Engledow and he saw this as his opportunity to get even with him on my behalf, so he wrote a letter back demanding to know why he was asking for a letter as I had already told him where I was and he wanted to know why he didn't believe me. He then added a few more comments about his opinions on Mr Engledow's teaching skills just for good measure. The next day, Mr Engledow told me that the Headmaster was dealing with my father's 'objectionable letter'. I shrugged and said I knew nothing about it. The following day, Dad received a letter from Mr Hopkins, which started by saying, 'I must say quite plainly that never before can I remember reading such an objectionable letter from the parent of a boy in my school…'

Dad opened and read the letter in front of me and I thought he was going to have a heart attack. He went into a sheer paroxysm of rage and bellowed, 'How dare he! Who does he think he is? If he thinks that letter was objectionable, wait till he sees my next one!'

He immediately reached for a piece of paper and I think I could literally see the sparks flying from the pen as he wrote back. It began,

Dear Sir,

I received your letter this morning and quite frankly, I was appalled. It appeared to me as if you rushed it out just to appease Mr Engledow, the parent's point of view did not matter. Mr Engledow told my son that you were dealing with 'that objectionable letter', coincidence you should use that word. He should have said nothing to my son who, after all, did not know what I had written; that is rather objectionable.

After a few more pleasantries of this sort, Dad finished up by saying,

> I, sir, have nothing to thank Mr Engledow for. He has caused me, indirectly, a lot of mental anguish. I am today a very sad man and receiving such a letter from a headmaster has certainly not improved matters.

Neither Mr Hopkins nor Mr Engledow ever mentioned the matter again, either to Dad or me. Funnily enough it reminded me of my last year at Rushmore when Dad had had the argument with the Head over my non-prize and the 11-plus result. What a way to finish up at both schools!

In the second year of sixth form, we were allowed some special privileges. One of these was the use of Room 24. Although we had a form room in the main building, there was also a basement room, set aside as a more casual common room for us in the house next door to the school at 24 Approach Road, where the caretaker lived. It was supposed to be used as a place for quiet study but I can't remember anyone ever actually studying in there. We used to go there when we didn't have any lessons and used it mainly to discuss sport or politics, listen to music and have a cup of coffee and a fag. I don't ever remember a teacher venturing down there, which is why we were left free to do much as we liked there.

At first, we used to listen to pop music, the Beatles especially, but one day Pete Scott brought in two Bob Dylan LPs, *The Freewheelin' Bob Dylan* and *The Times They Are a-Changin'*, and we were all converted in varying degrees to folk music. The records of singers like Bob Dylan and Joan Baez chimed precisely with our political view on the world. Many were about the fight for civil rights in America and, as time went on, about the Vietnam War. Thanks in part to the new wave of American protest singers, folk music as a whole began a revival in this country and a number of folk songs reached the Top 20. For a while, it was a big thing and many new folk clubs opened up, while the leading singers appeared on television. Folk music played a big part in politicising the youth of this country in the mid-sixties. I became a big fan of the whole scene and got very involved, not only with the protest movement but also with British and Irish traditional folk music. I started buying records and going to concerts and folk clubs. Eventually, I even became part of a folk duo – the Norman half of Robin and Norman – and appeared at a number of folk clubs in and around London and East Anglia (vocals, guitar and tin whistle).

At lunchtime, we would more often than not repair to the pub, not The Approach, as we didn't want any teachers seeing us, but to a pub just round the corner, the Prince of Wales. Here we'd usually have a half pint of brown, or if we had time and money it would sometimes stretch to a whole pint. One day, after saving up for some time, I decided I would try something a bit different. As it happened, I arrived later than the others at the pub that day and, as I walked in, Herb, who had got in the round for everyone, asked me what I wanted. 'It's okay,' I said, 'I'll get my own today.' So I went up to the bar and ordered a vodka and lime. It cost 2/6d and I paid for it with five sixpenny pieces. As I sat down at the table, the others all gave me funny looks until someone said, 'You flash git!' and we all laughed. After I drank it, I wished I'd stuck to the brown ale.

Although we were now in the sixth form and specialising in our A-levels, we still had a games afternoon at our sports ground. However, there were a couple of times when we missed the coach because we left the pub too late. On those occasions, we just went back to Room 24. None of the teachers ever said anything. I think they assumed, or maybe hoped, we'd missed games because we were studying.

It was during one of those afternoons in Room 24 after a longer-than-usual visit to the pub that we came up with a plan to kidnap Alan Oland. Alan was a bit of a loner and didn't really have many friends. He wasn't unpleasant or anything, but, no doubt with the assistance of some alcohol, we thought it would be a good idea to play a trick on him. It was agreed that Clive Smith, who had passed his driving test and sometimes came to school by car, would pick him up at the bus stop and offer him a lift to school. He would then drive him to the other side of Victoria Park, throw him out and make him walk back to school, by which time he would be very late.

On the appointed morning, a big mass of sixth formers waited at the school gate. Mr Engledow came out and asked what we were doing there. Clive said, 'Oland's late. I kidnapped him.' To his credit, Mr Engledow just laughed and said we could stay and wait. Alan eventually arrived to a big cheer and went off to report to the Headmaster for being late. Mr Hopkins solemnly wrote down in the late book, 'Alan Oland. Reason for being late: Kidnapped'. As it happened, Alan took it all in good part and saw the funny side of the whole incident. As, fortunately, did the Head and Mr Engledow.

Although I was thoroughly enjoying the social side of school life, I really had to consider what I was going to do when I left school, a day that was rapidly becoming imminent. I was fairly sure that I wasn't going to get good enough A-level grades to go to university, if indeed I actually passed any at all.

As the thought of going out to work straight from school didn't really appeal to me either, I opted for what was then seen as the next best option to university, teacher training college. I spoke to my teachers and my parents about this. My teachers readily agreed it was probably my best bet. Mum and Dad were a bit disappointed that I didn't feel I was going to get good enough grades to go to university, especially as John had gained his B.A. in English Literature at Cambridge, but in the end they agreed to support me.

At that time, the application form allowed you to apply for six colleges: two first choices and four second choices. My first choices were Borough Road, Isleworth, and Keswick Hall, on the outskirts of Norwich. The former because it had the best name as a teacher training college, the latter because it meant I would be able to go to speedway at Norwich. I suppose it was asking a bit much to be considered suitable for the best college in the country and, indeed, my application was turned down without even an interview.

Not long after sending off my form, however, I received a letter from Keswick Hall, asking me to come for an interview. On the appointed day, I set off for Liverpool Street station by bus to catch the train to Norwich. I had to go through three interviews and an oral English test – the only part of which I can remember now is that I was asked the meaning of undulating. I replied, 'Something that goes up and down,' and moved my hand in a wave motion to demonstrate what I meant. The woman interviewing me said, 'Every single person I have asked has done the same thing with their hand.'

One of the fellow interviewees I met on my visit to Norwich was Dave Gale, who was to become my best friend at college.

At the end of the day, I had no idea how I had done but about a week later I received a conditional offer of a place, the condition being that I gained at least one more O-level. I had four O-levels and the minimum entry requirement was five. Of course, an A-level would have been enough, but I wasn't confident I was going to pass any so I spoke to Mr Engledow and asked if he could suggest an O-level I might study, along with my A-levels. After some thought and discussion, we decided on the rather esoteric-sounding Greek Literature in Translation, as this was something that combined my liking for English and History. I started studying for this in January 1965, with just six months to complete what would normally be a two-year course. I had special lessons with Charlie Bowen, our Latin teacher, and I concentrated on getting this O-level. Now that I knew I only needed this to get to college, I took even less interest in my A-levels, giving up French altogether.

In the end, I got a grade C in Greek Literature and O-level passes in English and History, which meant I was on my way to Norwich, though there was a bit of a bombshell when it was announced later on that year that Norwich Speedway was to close and the stadium sold for a housing development. So I never did get to see speedway there!

CHAPTER TEN

MICK MCMANUS, *JUKE BOX JURY* AND BREAKING THE LAW

To start with, my elevation to grammar school didn't alter the general weekend routine, but, by the time 1960 came around and I was moving into my teenage years, the idea of doing the weekly shopping up Chatsworth Road appealed less and less to me and I decided to stay at home on Saturday mornings. It was on those occasions that for the first time I was really able to listen to pop music at home. *Saturday Skiffle Club*, introduced by Brian Matthew, had started on the *Light Programme* in 1957, but by 1959 had dropped 'Skiffle' from its title and was reaching an audience of something like five million listeners in its two-hour slot from 10am to 12 noon. It was exciting, listening to British singers such as Adam Faith, Marty Wilde, Billy Fury and Terry Dene, along with American rock stars like Gene Vincent, Eddie Cochrane, Bobby Darin and the Everly Brothers.

Pop and rock now began to play a much more important part in my musical life than Gilbert and Sullivan or Dad's other classical records. It was also about this time that we bought a new reel-to-reel tape recorder, a Belle, which played at the incredibly slow speed of 1 7/8 ips. But it did mean that I was able to record some of my favourite songs and singers off the wireless and play them at other times. Although I don't think Dad approved of my newfound musical taste, he nevertheless realised that I was now a teenager and he didn't interfere with my listening when he wasn't there, though he did draw the line at actually buying records or having to listen to it himself.

Sport on television in the early part of the afternoon continued as before, though it was now brought together under the heading of a brand-new programme called *Grandstand*, presented firstly by Peter Dimmock and then David Coleman. ITV also had its Saturday afternoon programme, *World of Sport*. This gradually became dominated by professional wrestling, with many of the leading wrestlers, such as Mick McManus, Jackie 'Mr TV' Pallo, Bert Royal, Billy Two Rivers, the Great Togo, Les Kellett, Vic Faulkner and George Kidd becoming household names as people tuned in in their millions to see these giants of the ring, cheering on the goodies and booing the baddies.

As well as on television, they appeared in theatres and halls round the country. Hackney Empire regularly featured wrestling bills, though it always seemed to be the same wrestlers appearing time after time. I lost count of the number of times I saw posters up around Hackney advertising 'Judo' Al Hayes v. 'Rebel' Ray Hunter. They must have got sick of the sight of each other! Nevertheless, people would flock to see them live whenever they appeared. As it happened, I wasn't all that keen on it myself but Dad was an avid fan. Of course, he knew that it wasn't real but for him that was half the fun, watching all the manufactured outrage when a foul went unpunished or the exaggerated staggering around the ring after a light tap and even the occasional assault by an incensed member of the public on the 'baddie'.

Dad had always been keen on wrestling since he was a teenager and used to go and see it in the halls around Aldgate. In fact, he loved it so much that for his first-ever date with Mum he thought he'd treat her to an evening of all-in wrestling, especially as the stars that particular night were Norman the Butcher and the Giant Anaconda. He felt this was the idyllic way to start a courtship. Sadly, Mum did not agree and, as soon as the first bout started, she jumped up from her seat and ran out. Dad told me many years later, 'The delicate art of this cultured sport was entirely lost on her,' before adding ruefully, 'It cost me a shilling as well.' It was just as well that Mum eventually forgave him or I'd never have been born!

The visits to Chingford also carried on. However, once we arrived at Nan and Grandpa's, I didn't stop long as I used to take a walk round to Aunt Julie's to meet up with my cousins, Wendy, Rita, John and Carol. They were all round about my age, Wendy and Rita just a little bit older, John and Carol a bit younger. Aunt Julie and her family had moved to Chingford from their prefab in Bethnal Green in the early 1950s and were now on the same estate as Nan and Grandpa, just a five-minute walk away.

This was another opportunity for me to listen to pop records, as Wendy and Rita were not hampered in this regard by their parents in the same way I was. Rita's favourite singer was Adam Faith and as soon as a new record of his came out she bought it. After staying for an hour or so, I would walk back, sometimes with Wendy and Rita, who would quite often bring a few of their records with them and play them on Nan's gramophone when we got back. Heaven knows what my grandparents thought of this intrusion on their normal Saturday night entertainment and telly, but they never seemed to object. I'm absolutely certain Dad wasn't too pleased but what could he say?

Aunt Clara used to like pop music as well. She was quite a bit younger than her brothers and sisters and in 1960 was only twenty-five years old as opposed to Dad, who was forty-five. Once the records were put on, Aunt Clara took charge and cleared away the chairs to make a space on the floor where we could jive. Not having had much practice at this new dance form, I'm afraid my early attempts weren't too successful. On one occasion, Grandpa gazed at my feeble efforts and remarked, 'You look more like a dancer's labourer than a dancer, Norman.'

When we didn't get to play records, usually we watched television and it was one evening in 1963 that I settled down to watch the first episode of a new science-fiction series called *Dr Who*, starring William Hartnell. Although I found it interesting, I have to say it did not grab my attention immediately and I watched it on and off over the next year or so, but if Rita and Wendy brought their records round they always took precedence.

One Saturday evening programme that combined the best of

both worlds was the BBC's *Juke Box Jury*, compered by David Jacobs, as this played new pop releases with a guest panel having to vote on whether it would be a hit or a miss. For some reason, Dad didn't seem to mind this programme. Maybe it was the competitive element or more likely it was because he was often amused by Nan's antics. She got right into the programme and if the panel didn't agree with her view there would be more than a few 'bloodys' and 'buggers' directed at the television.

ITV introduced a pop programme in the 1960s called *Thank Your Lucky Stars*, part of which, the 'Spin-a-Disc' section, followed a similar format to *Juke Box Jury*, where a guest D.J. and three teenagers reviewed three singles. It was here that Janice Nicholls first appeared and became famous for the catchphrase 'Oi'll give it foive' said in her strong Black Country accent.

Initially, Sundays also followed the normal pattern but this changed somewhat when Dad arrived home from work one evening and proudly announced, 'I passed my driving test today.' Mum and I looked at him in astonishment – we didn't even know he'd been learning to drive. After letting the initial shock sink in, he continued, 'So this Saturday we're going to buy a car.'

Good as his word, the following weekend he took me round to several second-hand car dealers in Hackney to help him look for a car. The one we finally settled on was a 1957 black Ford Anglia. Our first outing in it was to Chingford. As John was also at home, all four of us went. Much to my disappointment, as we got in the car, Dad said, 'John, you sit in the front, so you can watch and start learning how to drive.' So, rather grudgingly, I had to sit in the back on our first proper outing in the car. When we arrived at Nan's, Dad tooted the horn and Nan and Uncle Albert and his family came out to see us. Nan took one look and said, 'Lord and Lady bloody Muck, we are honoured.'

The car's registration plate read 284 KMP, but in keeping with Dad's penchant for nicknaming everyone and everything he decided to call it 'Arnold Pentecost', so that's how it was known to us all. Although owning a car didn't significantly change our everyday life, it did make a big difference at weekends and during holidays. For a start, we drove to Chingford every Saturday and, although Mum still visited her parents by bus, we always went to pick her up in the evening. It was because of this that I met my other grandpa for the first time. At this time I still knew nothing about his past and all I saw was a white-haired old man sitting in his armchair, always with the top button of his trousers undone, just watching television and saying nothing. Dad, of course, wouldn't speak to him and, after some brief pleasantries with Nan, we would be off; we never stayed longer than ten minutes at the most.

But it was our Sunday routine that was most altered by the arrival of the car as it was pressed into service to go places we would never have attempted to get to by public transport. These varied from beauty spots such as Hatfield Forest to historical places like Audley End, as well as some lesser-known seaside resorts, including Burnham-on-Crouch and Maldon. Our visit to Burnham-on-Crouch resulted in Dad involving us all in breaking the law! We went into a café and ordered some drinks, orange squash for me, tea for Mum and Dad, and ham sandwiches for all of us. The tea and orange came up very quickly but there was no sign of the sandwiches. Dad called the waitress over and asked where our sandwiches were.

She replied, 'They'll be ready soon.'

More time passed and we tried to hang out the drinks but the tea was getting cold and so, after finishing it and still with no sign of the sandwiches arriving, Dad said, 'Come on, let's go. I'm not waiting any longer.'

So we left the café without paying for the drinks… and still hungry.

Every Friday evening, Dad would have his tea and then say to me, 'Get the bucket filled up then.' This was the start of our weekly ritual of cleaning the car. Although he didn't take quite as much pride in our car as Old Daddy Flat Cap did in his, he nevertheless wanted it to be a credit to the Jacobs household, so off we went, carrying buckets of water up and down the path to clean all the London grime off before giving it a good polish. It might have been a labour of love for him, but I can't say I saw it in quite the same way myself.

Our local garage, Eleanor Motors, was on the corner of Chatsworth Road and Lea Bridge Road. This is where we always bought our petrol. There was no self-service then so the tank was filled up by the attendant. We always asked for 'four and four shots', which meant four gallons of petrol and four shots of Redex. I was never sure what the point of the Redex was, though I understood it had something to do with making the car run better, but I think it was more accepted folklore than really beneficial. It was supplied from a big dispenser next to the pumps.

Because the car was filled up by an attendant, Dad would

always give him a tip. However, I was unaware of this fact and one day I went with John just after he'd passed his driving test to get some petrol. Dad gave me £1 1s to pay for it. The price of a gallon of petrol was four shillings and eleven pence, which meant that four and four shots came to exactly £1, which is what the attendant asked for. So I gave him the £1 note and kept the coins. When we got home, I gave Dad back the shilling and he said, 'What's this? Why are you giving me back a shilling?'

Before I could answer, John put in, 'Norman didn't feel like giving him a tip.'

Why John couldn't have told me at the garage what the extra shilling was for, I don't know.

After having Arnold Pentecost for a few years, we sold him and bought a second-hand Ford Popular with the licence plate YGB 203. Somewhat predictably, it was nicknamed 'Yogi Bear' by Dad.

CHAPTER ELEVEN

THE COLDEST WINTER, GREEN SHIELD STAMPS AND DOUBLE DIAMOND

As we moved towards the end of the 1950s and through the 1960s, with all food now off rationing and the days of austerity inflicted by the War receding fast, a general increase in prosperity and living standards led to a tangible upturn in the ease and comfort with which most people in our position lived. For us, it meant we saw a number of changes to our prefab and the way we lived our everyday lives. The most important were the ones that helped Mum and saved her from some of the hardest parts of her job as a housewife.

Probably the first major labour-saving device we bought was a washing machine. Dad had seen an advert in the newspaper for the new Rolls-Razor washing machine and had sent off the coupon asking for more information. But it wasn't just information he got, as a couple of days later a salesman arrived, complete with a new twin tub washer drier, which he set up in the kitchen for us. It was something like half the price of the nearest equivalent Hotpoint or Hoover machine. The salesman told us they were able to do this as they sold direct to the public and not through shops. We could have it on hire purchase if we wanted, he added.

He was in and out of the house in less than half an hour and we had a new washing machine, bought for cash, as Dad didn't believe in hire purchase. Like a lot of people of his generation, he believed you should only buy something when you could afford it and not put yourself into debt. When the salesman had gone, Dad shook his head and said, 'I didn't think I could fall for sales patter like that.' He was very concerned that he had been taken in by the speed of it all and began to regret buying it.

On the other hand, Mum was delighted. 'It's just what I wanted,' she said. 'It looks ideal to me.'

Dad needn't have worried as the washing machine worked perfectly until we left the prefab several years later. At a stroke, the new washing machine made the copper and the mangle redundant and made things much easier for Mum.

The other big job she had was cleaning out the coal fire every morning in winter and getting it ready for the evening. This was dealt with when we bought a new electric fire to place in the hearth. No more raking out the ashes, no more polishing and blacking the grate, no more getting the bucket of coal in from the shed. It was just a matter of flicking the switch now.

Along with the labour-saving devices, some of our rising prosperity was spent acquiring goods for our leisure activities. We got a new 21" television, a new, much smaller radio and separate record player to take the place of the monster radiogram, giving us more space with no loss of quality (in fact, better quality) and the brand-new reel-to-reel tape recorder, mentioned earlier, which not only recorded off the radio but also allowed you to speak into it and then play your own voice back. Amazing!

But not everything made our lives easier. One Sunday morning, towards the end of December 1962, I got up out of bed to see everything outside completely covered in white. The snow had started just before I went to bed and was still coming down when I got up. And, judging by the depth, it hadn't stopped all night. Now inches thick, it was still falling.

'Talk about "Rupert looked out on the dismal scene,"' said Dad, referring to the line from my old Rupert Bear annuals we still frequently quoted.

There was hardly any let up during the day, and the following morning, which was a Monday, Dad shook me awake early on and said, 'Come on, we'll have to get that path clear.'

Although I was on school holiday, Mum and Dad were both due to go into work. Fortunately, it had stopped snowing at last and Dad and I got kitted up with warm clothes and wellies, got the garden spade and rake out of the shed and shovelled away the snow onto the grass. All along our row of prefabs, the other occupants were doing the same while across the road there was a similar scene. It seemed that everyone was out clearing the snow away. The road itself was covered in snow and I said to Dad, 'How are you going to get to work?'

'I'll have to drive, won't I?' he replied stoically. 'Come on, help me clear the snow and ice off the car.'

The car itself was under so much snow you could hardly make out the shape but we cleared enough off for Dad to be able to see out the windows. After shovelling a bit of snow away from in front of the wheels, he got in, pulled the choke out and turned the key in the ignition. Amazingly, it roared into life first time of asking. He put it into gear and slowly drove off down the road, sliding and skidding as he went. I thought he was never going to make it and I was a bit worried about what would happen but he continued driving until I saw him turn the slight corner into Powerscroft Road and then he was gone from sight.

Not long after he went, Mum got all her winter clothes on and trundled off up Chatsworth Road to the toy factory just as it started to snow again.

Little did we know then that all this shovelling, sliding, skidding, winter clothes and going to work in the snow was to become our way of life for more than two months as our new electric fire was tested to its limits. From December 1962 to March 1963, Great Britain suffered the coldest and most prolonged winter since the seventeenth century. The bad winter had in fact begun early in December when thick smog descended on London. As it turned out this was the last of the pea-soupers to affect the city before the results of the Clean Air Act finally kicked in.

A few days later, there were a couple of days of snow, but the big freeze itself began on 22 December. Although bitterly cold, the snow did not start falling until late on Boxing Day, followed by a blizzard of Arctic proportions on the nights of 29 and 30 December. From that point on, there was a continual covering of snow on the ground for over two months and yet, throughout it all, with plenty more heavy snowfalls and thick snow and ice lying on the ground, we managed to carry on. I don't think I missed school once during that period, though I was late on several occasions and we were sent home at lunch-time a number of times. As I wore my wellies to school every day, I had to take my shoes with me in my satchel.

Meanwhile, Mum and Dad continued to struggle into work every day, though there were a couple of times when Dad came home very late and said he'd had to abandon the car somewhere along the route as the snow was too deep. Which meant not only had he had to walk home in a blizzard but also he'd have to walk out in the snow the next day to find the car and hope it was all right.

We still managed to get to Chingford and London Bridge at the weekends. Most days I was still able to go out and see my friends or they were able to come to me. A lot of effort was put into keeping the roads clear, both by the authorities and by people themselves. We continued to get up and out early every morning to shovel the latest ice and snow from the path, as did all our neighbours. Nowadays, a few hours of snow, never mind months, seems to land the whole country in crisis.

The main thing that did suffer nationally was the football programme. Some clubs were unable to play any matches for over two months. It was during this period that the football pools companies introduced the Pools Panel to adjudicate on what the result would have been had the match been played. Rugby union, rugby league and horse racing all suffered in the same way.

It wasn't until 6 March 1963 that the overnight temperature rose above freezing for the first time, the snow began to thaw and within a few days it was all gone. Life returned to normal.

Although I tended not to go out shopping so much with my parents up Chats once I was into my teenage years, there were occasions during the holidays when I still accompanied Mum to Mare Street, mainly to go to Woolworths, though I still had to put up with her insistence on visiting Marks & Spencer.

During the 1960s, a number of changes came to Mare Street, the first being the opening of a new American-style restaurant. Until then, whenever we went to Mare Street, we normally stopped for elevenses, tea and cake in the A.B.C. Tea Shop. A.B.C. stood for Aerated Bread Company, though we often referred to it as the 'Aeriated' Bread Company, which had the completely different meaning to a Cockney of being overexcited. This was a popular chain of teashops at the time, rivalling Lyons Corner Houses.

The first time I saw this new restaurant, I thought it looked very bright and welcoming, as opposed to the universal black and white decor of the A.B.C., so I said to Mum, 'Can we go in there and see what it's like?'

'I don't see why not,' she agreed and we ordered something called a Wimpy.

It was a hamburger, a delicacy we had never had before, and seemed to be a real taste of America. I thought it was absolutely delicious and from then on whenever we went to Mare Street we'd look in for a Wimpy, progressing to various Wimpy meals, which often included a 'bender'. It was all new to me. It's hard to imagine youngsters not knowing what an American hamburger is today.

Another new shop was a record shop that opened near Woolworths. It was here, at the age of thirteen, that I bought my first record. Was it Elvis Presley? Del Shannon? The Everly Brothers? Sadly not! It was 'Please Mr Custer' by Charlie Drake. In mitigation of this lapse of taste, I think I should point out that the record did, in fact, reach number 12 in the British charts, so it wasn't just me.

Although not new, a big change took place at Sainsbury's as it was turned into a supermarket. In fact, Sainsbury's was the pioneer of supermarkets in this country and followed a visit to the United States by the company chairman, Alan Sainsbury, where he saw for himself the benefits of this type of shop for the customer and realised it was the future. As I mentioned earlier, both Victor Value and Tesco had already been converted into small self-service shops in Chatsworth Road but they were nothing like the scale of the Sainsbury's in Mare Street. One thing it did mean, though, was that there was no more butter patting or sugar poured out into conical bags. It was all in packets straight off the shelf now. The only grocer's shop in Hackney now selling groceries in the old-fashioned way was the Home and Colonial Stores in Chatsworth Road, but we hardly ever went in there.

One thing Victor Value and Tesco did, however, that Sainsbury's didn't do was to give away trading stamps. Victor Value was first with their 'King Korn' stamps, but it was when Tesco started issuing 'Green Shield Stamps' that this form of customer inducement really took off. The idea was that whenever you bought an item in Tesco you were given so many Green Shield Stamps depending on the value of your purchases. These stamps were stuck in special books. Green Shield issued a catalogue stating how many books were needed for you to trade in for different items; these could range from very cheap items for just one or two books to more expensive items costing hundreds of books. You could order from the catalogue and have the item delivered or take your books to a Green Shield Stamp redemption centre. Our nearest centre was in Dalston and we often went there to trade in our books for small household items that we probably would not otherwise have purchased. For a while, these trading stamps, as well as 'S&H Pink Stamps', a similar scheme backed by Fine Fare Supermarkets, were very popular and many people saved up their stamps to be able to obtain goods they might not normally have been able to afford.

It wasn't just Tesco who gave away these stamps, as many petrol filling stations and other smaller shops also participated in the scheme, but Tesco was by far their biggest customer and, when the supermarket chain pulled out in the late 1970s, it spelt the end for Green Shield Stamps, with the centres eventually becoming Argos catalogue shops.

What with staying on at school a couple of days a week and homework practically every night, something I hadn't encountered at Rushmore, I didn't get to see much children's television on my return home from school. On the brief occasions I was able to watch, I saw some new programmes take the place of old favourites. *Blue Peter* started in October 1958 and *Animal Magic*, starring Johnny Morris, in 1962. There were a number of new cartoon shows from the States, including

Huckleberry Hound, featuring Yogi Bear, and *The Flintstones*, which I can remember seeing for the first time one evening while Dad was putting up the Christmas decorations. Another new cartoon show imported from America was *Top Cat*, which was called *The Boss Cat* in this country, even though the name Boss Cat was never used at any time during the programme itself and the main character was always known as Top Cat (or T.C.). The reason for this bizarre titling was that there was a brand of cat food called Top Cat on the market and the BBC didn't want to be seen to be advertising it.

In any case, as I grew into my teenage years, many of the children's programmes were now too young for me and as I was able to stay up later I looked forward to some of the early evening programmes. These included sitcoms such as *Bootsie and Snudge*, a spin-off from *The Army Game*, *The Charlie Drake Show* ('Hello, my darlings!') and *Here's Harry*, starring Harry Worth, which became most famous for its opening title sequence showing Harry stopping in the street to perform an optical trick next to a shop window in which he would raise one arm and one leg. This was reflected in the window, giving the impression that he was able to levitate. Along with most of the rest of the country I suppose, my friends and I tried to copy this when we were out on the street. In fact, the action became known as 'doing a Harry Worth'. There were also a number of comedy variety shows starring British icons of comedy, including Tommy Cooper and Morecambe & Wise.

There were some new exciting adventure series such as *The Avengers*, starring Patrick Macnee as John Steed, which after one or two series morphed into an eccentric and surreal fantasy escapade with Macnee supported by a succession of intelligent and self-assured female assistants including Honor Blackman, Diana Rigg and Linda Thorson. Another new stylish adventure series, *Danger Man*, starring Patrick McGoohan, also eventually turned into an even more bizarre flight of fancy when McGoohan became *The Prisoner* – 'I am not a number!' It seemed that, while, on the one hand, television was getting away from the comfortable middle-class entertainment of the 1950s by putting on more down-to-earth gritty dramas, *Coronation Street*, *Z-Cars* and *Armchair Theatre*, for example, there was a balancing movement right at the other end of the scale, taking the viewer into a completely illusory and dreamlike world. Perhaps this was reflective of the fact that more and more people were able to afford televisions and both the BBC and ITV realised they had to cater for all tastes rather than the limited numbers of reasonably well-off people who could afford it in the 1950s and also that there was now competition for viewers.

At the age of about fourteen, I started going to a youth club in Bow with Herb, as it was quite near where he lived. It was attached to the local Methodist Church and run by the minister, the Revd. David Monckton. The club itself was not used to push Methodism or any other form of religion and welcomed youngsters of all or no religions. It was a place where we could play table tennis, snooker, pool, darts or just sit around and chat; there was also a small kitchen attached.

Not long after I joined, I was told it was my turn to make the tea and coffee, so I went into the kitchen to boil the kettle, something I had done many times at home, but, horror of horrors, it was a gas kettle and only having electricity in the prefab I had never come across this way of boiling a kettle before. I knew that you had to light the gas on the stove and put the kettle on it, but I had heard stories of gas explosions and I was very wary of the whole process. What I did therefore was to turn on the gas, light a match and then turn the gas down as low as I could before trying to light it to avoid blowing up the whole youth club and everyone in it. However, what kept happening was that I turned it down so low that the gas went out altogether. I must have got through a boxful of matches before I decided that I had to be brave, turn the gas on and just light it. To my great relief, all that happened was the gas lit and I was able to boil the kettle. No big explosion and the youth club managed to survive. Fortunately, no one came into the kitchen to see what was taking me so long.

The other good thing about the club was that it brought us into contact with girls. Apart from some of my cousins, I hadn't really seen any girls close up to speak to since Junior School. After a few weeks, we started to feel part of the club and became friendly with many of the other members. One evening, as we were leaving, one of the older boys, Don, said to Herb and me, 'We usually go down the pub after club. Do you want to come with us?'

Somewhat naively, I said, 'We can't go there, we're only fifteen.'

Herb gave me a withering look and said, 'Well, you don't have to come but I'm going.'

But of course, I did have to go! So we trooped across to the pub and, without asking, Don ordered us a pint of Red Barrel each. Red Barrel was a hugely popular drink in the 1960s and something of a cultural phenomenon. If you went into a Watney's pub, you were expected to buy Red Barrel. The strange thing was that, as well as being so popular, it was almost de rigueur to deride it and complain that it was too fizzy or had no flavour. Its great rival was Ind Coope's Double Diamond, which seemed to suffer the same fate of being universally popular while at the same time generally criticised.

This was my first alcoholic drink and I had heard stories of people being sick with their first pint so I drank it quite slowly and frankly wasn't really impressed by it. I would have preferred a glass of lemonade but of course I didn't dare say so.

My night of growing up wasn't quite over yet, however, as, just after we arrived, I was a little taken aback when Herbert took a packet of cigarettes out of his pocket and offered me one. I wasn't sure what to do as I had never had one before, but I didn't want to seem odd so I took one, though, as it happens, a couple of the others refused, so I wouldn't have been the only one not smoking. Just like with alcohol, I had heard stories about people having their first cigarette and choking or being sick so I was a bit apprehensive, but it was too late to go back now and, when Herbert lit it for me, I took my first drag and proceeded to smoke the whole cigarette without choking or feeling sick. Not only that but I actually quite enjoyed it. It was a different but pleasant sensation.

Although I don't think the minister approved, our visits to the pub, the Lady Franklin, after the club became a regular part of the evening. It was during one of these after-club drinks that I at last summoned up the courage to talk to Minna Sheppard, a girl I had quite fancied for some time, but, having had no real experience with girls, had not really had the guts to speak to before, at least not in a chatting-up way. The evening went well as she responded encouragingly to my stilted attempts at small talk and I thought to myself, I really have got to ask her out the next time I see her.

There was a big pop concert, starring Del Shannon, Johnny Tillotson and The Springfields, coming up at the Walthamstow Granada in a couple of weeks. As it happened, the Walthamstow Granada was next door to our school clothing outfitter, Henry Taylor, in Hoe Street and I had to buy some new school shirts. So, after getting the shirts, I went to the box office and bought two tickets for the concert.

The following week, as usual we went to the pub and I decided that it had to be tonight or never, so armed with my two tickets I sat down next to Minna. I had never asked a girl out before and I felt very nervous, especially as there were so many other people around. Suppose she said no? Worse, suppose she laughed at me in front of our friends? This called for a bit of strategy to try to get her on her own. As there were so many of us, it had become a tradition to take weekly turns in buying the drinks as if we all bought a round every time we went we'd not only be there all night but we would probably have found it difficult to stay upright!

We normally stayed for two or three pints and, as it happened, this week it was Herb's turn to buy the first round and mine to get the second. So I came up with a plan inside my head that when it was my turn to get them in I'd ask Minna if she'd help me get the drinks and ask her out when we were alone at the bar. At least this put the dreaded moment off for a while and I sat slowly sipping my first drink. I didn't take much part in the conversation going on around me as words kept going round and round in my head. 'Would you like to come out with me?', 'I've got two tickets…', 'I like you, Minna, so I was wondering…' What was I going to say exactly? Suddenly I heard Herb saying to me, 'You're smoking a lot tonight.'

I realised then that the other thing I was doing was almost chain smoking. As soon as I'd put one cigarette out, I was lighting another. (I was now buying my own cigarettes, though I was only really smoking when I went out with my friends.) I smiled and then Herb said, 'Drink up, it's your turn. Everyone's gasping.'

I noticed that most people had finished their drinks and, although I still had some way to go, I said, 'Okay,' and got up slowly to go to the bar.

My heart was pounding and my knees turned to jelly and I thought perhaps I could phone her. For some reason just at that point, she looked at me and smiled. I thought to myself, 'No, it's got to be now or never,' so I said to her, 'Come and help me with the drinks, Minna?'

She nodded and came to the bar with me. I ordered the round and turned to her. There was a pause while I metaphorically took a deep breath and eventually blurted out, 'Minna, I don't suppose you'd like to come out with me next Sunday, would you? I've got two tickets for Del Shannon at the Granada.'

Her head shot up as though I'd given her an electric shock. 'Del Shannon,' she squealed excitedly, 'I'd love to! He's my favourite. How did you get tickets?'

My mind was reeling. Did she really say, 'I'd love to'? All

I could say by way of a reply was: 'You would?' Just then the drinks arrived and we took them back to the table.

'Norman's taking me to see Del Shannon next week,' she announced as soon as we got back to the table. 'I can't believe it. I love him!' There was a spontaneous 'oooo' from everyone. 'No, not Norman,' she said, 'Del Shannon.'

Even that slight put-down didn't dampen my spirits and I felt on cloud nine. The first girl I'd asked out and she'd said yes!

The sequel to this wasn't so good, however. I was used to Minna wearing very casual clothes at the club, mostly black, and I thought she looked very sexy in a sweater and jeans. We'd arranged to meet at a bus stop near where she lived, as for some reason she didn't want me to call at her house, but when she turned up I had to look twice to make sure it was her as she was wearing a dress. But that wasn't the problem and nor was the large feather boa she was also wearing: it was her make-up. She had put gallons of the stuff on her face. In particular, I found the heavy green eye-liner a huge turn-off. She just wasn't the same girl! I expect she'd done it to look nice for me and Del Shannon but I actually felt quite embarrassed being with her. Being in something of a daze, we hardly spoke going to the concert, though once we were there we did manage some light, if stilted, conversation and, on the way back, we managed a brief discussion about the show. When we got off the bus, I said, 'I'll see you then.'

She took hold of my hand and said, 'Aren't you going to kiss me goodnight then?'

It was something that had worried me before I came out. Having never been out with a girl I wasn't sure of the protocol of kissing on the first date. But now, I didn't really want to kiss her anyway. However, I said, 'Oh yes, of course,' and we kissed very briefly on the lips. Then I said, 'I've got to go. See you.' And I scooted off as fast as I respectably could.

When I got home, I felt terrible. My first date and it had been a disaster from my point of view. The problem was I really did like Minna when she was herself, but all the make-up and fancy clothes wasn't her, I felt.

Incidentally, it's probably a real sign of the times that I worried about kissing on a first date. This was one of the things we used to discuss in the playground as well as the other weighty matter of should you go all the way before you were married, even if you were going steady. Perhaps the early sixties was the last time such conversations took place before the sexual revolution of the late sixties as the contraceptive pill became more widely available and there was generally a much freer attitude towards sex with the hippie era of free love.

We met again the following week at the club when she was once again dressed in her black sweater and jeans. After the meeting, I took her to one side and said, 'Can we go to a different pub, just the two of us?'

She gave me an old-fashioned look and said, 'I didn't think you'd want to speak to me again after last Sunday.'

'Yes, I'm sorry about that,' I replied. 'That's why I want to talk to you alone.'

So, to the knowing nods and winks plus a few coarse comments from our friends, we walked off to another pub, a little further away. When we got there, I said, 'I'm sorry about last week, but to be honest I was a bit shocked by your

228

appearance. I'd really like to go out with you again,' I added, 'but I like you just as you are now.'

Much to my relief, she smiled and just said, 'Okay.'

We went out together a few more times and she never again wore bright-green eye-liner, but in spite of this we were never really able to put that first date behind us and the relationship didn't last very long as we didn't really have a lot in common. For one thing, she didn't like any form of sport. Can you believe it? Nevertheless, she was my first proper girlfriend.

After a couple of years at the club, the Minister started a new section for eight to twelve year olds and put Herb and me in charge of it. This used to take place earlier in the evening on the same night as the youth club, which didn't give much time to get our homework done on those evenings. It was generally enjoyable and made me feel that perhaps my decision to go to teacher training college might have been the right choice.

It was about this time that we started writing our novel, *Lilo Schlieberger Down South*. We used to meet, just the two of us, in the Lady Franklin on a separate night to club night and over a pint or two of brown and mild and maybe a barley wine and several cigarettes add a few pages each week. The novel began something like this,

Her frail naked disease-ridden form lay on the bed. Her life slowly ebbing away. 'Sam,' she cried. Sam knelt down by the bed and prayed. The smell of her decomposing body mixed fragrantly with the smell of the burnt greens in the kitchen. Sam knew that she had gone to meet her maker. Whether it was God or Satan he didn't know, but he knew she had gone to meet her maker. She was dead! But she had not always been like this. She was born of meagre parents, one of each sex…

We continued writing this book on and off for the next five years or so. It was always a mystery to us why some publisher did not see its potential as a bestseller and snap it up…

Going to the club was the start of regularly going out in the evenings. As my teens wore on, I had little enthusiasm for staying in and watching television and I spent a lot of time going out with friends, either to sporting events, folk clubs, political meetings or just down the pub. When we went out to the pub, we didn't have a regular haunt – apart from the Lady Franklin on club night – as there were many pubs in Hackney, so we used to frequent different ones all over the borough. At that time, all of them had at least two bars, the saloon bar and the public bar. We always went into the public bar – it was a bit cheaper because it wasn't quite so comfortable. For example, whereas the saloon bar had carpets on the floor, the public bar usually just had sawdust. The chairs round the tables in the public bar were bog standard wooden ones, whereas in the saloon bar they would be upholstered and have cushions. As well as drinking, putting the world to rights and talking about girls, we used to play darts a lot.

Sport still played a big part in my life and that of my friends, particularly John but also Herb. This was especially true at the weekends and in the holidays but also during term time. At Rushmore, nearly everyone was a Leyton Orient supporter, as their stadium wasn't far away, but with a wider catchment area there was a bigger variety of supported teams at Parmiter's, especially West Ham, Spurs and Arsenal. Herb was a keen Gunners fan and we went to Highbury several times to see them play. The only time I went to White Hart Lane to see Spurs was a midweek game when we were supposed to be at school. This was in January 1963. Spurs were the leading team in the old First Division in the early 1960s, having won the league in 1961 and the F.A. Cup in 1962. One of their biggest rivals was Burnley, who had finished runners-up in both the league and cup in 1962. The third round of the 1962/63 F.A. Cup drew these two teams together with ties due to be played on 5 January 1963. However, due to the big freeze, only three matches were actually played on that day, some not taking place until March. The Spurs–Burnley match, however, took place on Wednesday, 16 January. It was the most important match of the round and, in fact, was a repeat of the 1961/62 Cup Final. John, who was a diehard Spurs supporter, and I thought it was too good to miss, even if we were supposed to be at school. Several other boys in our class thought so too so we decided to bunk off school to see it.

Although it began to snow a little, a group of us left school at lunchtime and took the train from nearby Cambridge Heath Railway Station to White Hart Lane. By the time we reached the stadium, the snow had stopped and the match went ahead. It was a terrific game and, even though we were fully expecting some punishment the following day, most of us thought it was worth it. Most of us except the Spurs supporters that is, as Burnley romped to a convincing 3–0 victory. On the way home, John, who normally had a very cheery disposition, worked himself up into a right old state, complaining bitterly,

'Well, that wasn't worth getting fucking detention for! I wish I'd never gone. Spurs were fucking useless!' He went on and on about his team, pulling every single player to bits, berating them for their shortcomings and eventually dismissing the whole team as 'fucking wankers'. He then lapsed into a long silence and refused to say any more. I had never seen him in this sort of mood before. Even trying to change the subject brought no response from him and he just sat on the train staring darkly at the floor. Although I felt a bit sorry for my friend, I have to say that I thought, on balance, it probably was worth getting detention for – it had been such a brilliant match.

The next day, we arrived at school waiting to be summoned to see our form teacher, who was now Mr Hume, or even worse, the Head, but nothing happened. No one said anything. It was all a bit puzzling. Eventually, I asked Murray, who was not a football fan and therefore had not been to the match, if anyone had noticed we were missing yesterday afternoon. 'Of course not,' he said, 'we all got sent home just after lunch because there was another blizzard.' Result! Something good had come from that freezing winter at last, although John still wasn't in complete agreement with that sentiment.

Cricket also continued to figure high on my list and, as I got older, I was able to travel further afield to see it, going to Lord's and the Oval several times as well as Leyton. And a new sport, Ten Pin Bowling, was introduced from America in 1960. As it happened, the first bowling alley to open in this country was at Stamford Hill, just a short bus ride away. John and I decided to try it out not long after it opened. Very bright and brash, it seemed typically American and we loved it. We started going fairly regularly. Stamford Hill Bowling Alley stood on the site of a former cinema. Sadly, in some ways, this was just the start of the trend towards cinemas closing down and being replaced by bowling alleys. Cinema audiences were dropping everywhere, largely as a result of people staying in to watch television. At the time, we weren't concerned about this as we became keen on bowling.

Also in 1960, while I was still twelve, I started going to see a sport that was to become an all-consuming passion. Back in the late 1940s and early 1950s, Dad and John used to go to speedway at Harringay every week, so, although I was deemed too young to go myself, I heard a lot about it from them. It was at this period that speedway rivalled football, with tracks such as Wembley and West Ham attracting crowds of over 50,000 on a regular basis, but, during the 1950s, speedway declined and by the end of the decade there were very few tracks left around the country and only one in London at Wimbledon.

I had remained interested in the sport to the extent of following results in the newspapers and when I was riding my bike round the fields at the back of the prefab I pretended to be one of the top riders of the day, in particular Harringay's Split Waterman or West Ham's Aub Lawson, mainly because I liked their glamorous-sounding names.

So, although I had never actually seen any speedway live, I was steeped in its tradition. In fact, I was named after a speedway rider, Norman Parker, the Wimbledon captain. Many years later, Mum told me how this came about. When John was born, Dad went off to register his name without even consulting her, as it was Jewish tradition that the firstborn son would be named after his father's father, which in this case was John. When it came to me, the tradition was that I should be named after the mother's father, so I should have been William, but Mum, who had never forgiven Dad for not even asking her about John's name, said she didn't want to name me William and really didn't care what I was called. It was at this point that John suggested naming me Norman. Although he went to Harringay every week, he was, for some reason, a Belle Vue (Manchester) supporter. Their captain was Jack Parker, Norman's brother, so he reasoned if it was good enough for his hero to have a brother called Norman, he should have one too. As Mum wasn't too bothered, she agreed, so Norman I became.

At the end of 1959, there was a small revival in speedway and a number of old tracks returned, including New Cross. Dad always used to buy the *Evening News* on his way home from work and, one Wednesday evening in May 1960, I saw an article about that night's meeting at New Cross, a Britannia Shield match against Norwich. I looked up and said to Dad, 'Can we go?' Much to my surprise, he said, 'Yes.' New Cross wasn't far away by car, about half an hour through the Rotherhithe Tunnel, so off we went.

When we got there, we bought a programme and on scanning through it I noticed that the very first race amazingly brought together the two heroes from my bike-riding days, Split Waterman, now New Cross captain, and Aub Lawson, now with Norwich. It was a terrific race, which Lawson just managed to win. Watching these latter-day black leather-clad gladiators hurtling round the track at impossible angles, spraying flying cinders behind them, handlebars almost touching and seemingly on the verge of crashing at every corner was incredibly thrilling. And from then on I was hooked.

Very soon we got pally with a family who sat near where we did. Naturally, they all received their nicknames from Dad. Chief character among them was 'Fuzz', so-called because he had fuzzy hair. He spoke very slowly and was not the sharpest knife in the drawer. His friend was called El, who was the complete opposite. Sharp as a razor, he spoke at a million miles an hour. His mother was more interested in the refreshments than the racing and got up several times during the evening to go to the little tea stall. She was known as 'Mrs Cups of Tea' and, finally, there was Fuzz's father, whom we called 'The Authority' as he knew everything there was to know about speedway. People would come up to him from all over the stadium to ask him questions. He never failed to give them an answer, even to the most obscure enquiry.

Eventually, more London tracks reopened, including, in 1963, Hackney Wick, which was the other side of Hackney Marshes. It took me about twenty minutes to walk there so I became a regular. The following year, West Ham also reopened and I went there every week as well. By the time I was eighteen, I was going to speedway twice a week most weeks and sometimes three if there was a good match on at Wimbledon. My friend John also became a keen speedway fan so we used to go to all the meetings together, even going to Wembley when they put on big meetings, such as the World Championship Final.

CHAPTER TWELVE

MILITARY PICKLE AND THE MOULIN ROUGE

The first major outing for our new car came when we used it for our summer holiday in 1959. From 1950 to 1958, we had always gone by coach to a holiday camp. This time, with the freedom the car gave us, we decided to tour the West Country, stopping off at guesthouses for bed and breakfast wherever the fancy took us. Our first stop was Gloucester, where we met my uncle Jim and his wife Audrey. Uncle Jim was Mum's brother and this was the first and last time I ever saw him. We then went round Somerset, Devon, Cornwall and Dorset, finishing up with a look at Stonehenge on the way home. This was in the days when you could walk freely among the stones. I even had my photograph taken sitting on top of one of them.

For the most part, the car behaved well. The only hairy

moment we had was when we were trying to get up Porlock Hill, in Somerset, a 1 in 4 gradient. We just about struggled up in first gear; it seemed to take forever. I don't think 1950s family cars were made to take this sort of thing in their stride as they are today.

For the next few years, our car took us on touring holidays around the country as we went to Wales (North and South), the Lake District and Scotland. Our trip to North Wales was probably the most memorable. This was in the year following our West Country adventure, where we had had no difficulty in booking overnight bed and breakfast as we went. We decided that our first stop would be Colwyn Bay and because of our previous year's experience we agreed that we wouldn't just take the first B&B we came to but could afford to be selective. So we started off in optimistic mood and weren't too fazed when the first few guesthouses we came to were full, but, as time went on and still no rooms were to be found, we began to get a bit apprehensive so we went along to the Tourist Information Office and asked where we might be able to find bed and breakfast for the night. The woman behind the counter shook her head and blew her cheeks out. 'There won't be any vacancies this time of year,' she told us. 'The best thing you can do would be to go out a few miles and see if you can find anything.'

So we got back in the car and drove a little way, coming to a small village called Mochdre. We could see a number of guesthouses, so we started again, but same result. Then, just as we were losing hope for the night and having visions of sleeping in the car, we saw a house a little way up a hill with a 'Vacancies' sign outside. We knocked on the door and asked if there were any rooms available and the landlady said, 'Yes, I have a couple left.' Were we relieved! No thought now of being choosy and not taking the first B&B we came across. I think it could have been the stables out the back and we'd have taken it.

We were so chastened by the experience and so happy with the place we'd found that we abandoned the idea of touring and decided to remain there for the whole week of our holiday. As it happened, we needn't have worried as we had a very nice stay. The rooms were very comfortable and the breakfasts excellent. There was an added bonus in that the landlady's father kept us entertained at breakfast with tales of his army days dating back to the First World War and bemoaning the fact that you couldn't buy Military Pickle any more, as apparently it had been his favourite breakfast accompaniment when he was young. He apologised to us every single morning that there was none available for ours. On our last day, we went shopping in Station Road, the main shopping street of Colwyn Bay, for some presents to take home and there, on display in the window of a grocer's shop, were jars of Hayward's Military Pickle. We bought one and, as we were leaving the bed and breakfast, we gave it to the old man. I have never seen anyone so grateful in my whole life. He was absolutely speechless and his jaw just dropped. It was as if we had performed some miracle, magicking it up from thin air and bringing him the one thing that would make his life complete. We didn't like to tell him that Military Pickle was freely available – and probably had been for many years – in a shop just a few miles away.

So, using Mochdre as our base, we drove out to a different place each day. It was while doing this that we took a ride on the world's first commercial hovercraft in its initial year of service. For our trip out one day, we decided to visit the seaside resort of Rhyl. When we got there, we went down on to the beach, where the hovercraft was due to take off for Hoylake in Cheshire.

The steward was standing outside, shouting, 'Just three seats left. We're about to leave. If anyone wants to board, hurry up! One-way tickets only.'

'Come on, let's get on,' said Dad to Mum and me and started running down the beach.

Mum and I held back and I said, 'It's just one way, how will we get back?'

Dad, still going as fast as he could and very conscious of what was at stake, shouted back, 'We'll deal with that when we get there. This is our chance to be a part of history.'

So we got our one-way tickets and got on. It was a bit of a strange experience, skimming over land and sea, something few people had done before. And it was made even more odd by the fact that all seats faced backwards. There was also a powerful smell of petrol, so it wasn't a wholly pleasant experience but when we landed we each got a certificate to show we'd ridden on the world's first hovercraft in its first year of service. After arriving in Hoylake, we had to get a train to Liverpool, another train to Crewe and then a bus back to Rhyl before driving back to our digs. We got back very late and practically the whole day had been spent travelling, but Dad had been right and it was worth it to play a role in a small piece of history.

With the 1960s being a time of growing affluence among working-class families, more and more people were starting to go abroad for their holiday. And we were no exception. Although

240

we continued touring Great Britain in our car, we now started to take a second week's holiday to enable us to go to Europe. We took our first foreign holiday in 1960, a coach tour to Bruges, Brussels and Paris. Dad particularly loved the Belgian part of the holiday as we drove through many of the places he had been stationed in or had visited during the War and he spent a lot of time pointing out various sites to us and reminiscing about them. For me, the most interesting thing I found about Belgium was the enormous size of the chip portions they served up with every meal and the fact they smothered them with mustard pickle.

When we arrived in Paris, our guide told us that he had arranged an optional excursion to a show at the Moulin Rouge that evening and said he would be passing round a brochure explaining what sort of show we could expect to see if we went. As the brochure came round, I caught a glimpse of what it contained by looking through the gap in the seat backs while the couple in front thumbed through it. What I managed to see showed mostly scantily dressed and semi-naked women with large fans or kicking up their legs, dancing on a stage. When the couple in front passed it back to Mum, who was sitting next to me, she said to me, 'Would you like to have a look?' So, did I? I was dying to have a look, but I just felt so embarrassed sitting next to Mum that I said, 'No, it's all right.' So Mum passed it back to Dad, who was sitting behind next to another man. They seemed to take a long time scanning the pages and in truth I was a bit shocked and felt slightly uncomfortable – I'd never thought of my Dad as having any interest in women other than my mum. I suppose it was the first time it had ever occurred to me that Dad was a man as well as my dad, and might take an interest in scantily clad women. After all, he was in his forties now and to me a bit old for that sort of thing! As it happened, he didn't think it would be very suitable for me to go to the Moulin Rouge at my tender age so we opted out of the excursion, but I expect he wouldn't have minded going.

The following day, while leaving Paris to get back to Calais for the ferry, we stopped in a small town for a coffee break. The guide told us to be back in half an hour and if anyone wasn't back then the coach would go without them. On our way back to the coach, we passed two members of our party walking away in the opposite direction. At the appointed time for leaving, the two men still weren't back, so the guide said, 'Well, I did warn everyone. We will just have to go without them.'

Dad got up and said, 'We've just seen them, they can't be far away. I'll go and get them,' and promptly walked off the coach to look for them. As he turned the corner, the men came back round a different corner and got on the coach. At this, the guide said, 'Right, we'll have to go now.'

Now it was Mum's turn. 'You can't go,' she said, 'you know my husband has gone off to look for these two. He'll be back in a minute.'

'Sorry,' said the guide, 'you were all warned.'

'I can't go without my husband!' Mum yelled at him.

'Well, you'll have to get off as well then,' was all the guide could say.

By now, I was feeling really panicky. I couldn't let the coach drive off without us, so I went to the door and stood with one foot on the step and the other on the pavement. I was praying the coach wouldn't start off but I thought he wouldn't dare with me in this position. The guide moved towards me and Mum screamed at him, 'Don't you dare touch my boy!'

Just then, I could see Dad coming back up the road. Was I relieved! After he'd got back on, the guide gave us all a lecture about how it was important we leave on time to keep to our schedule. Mum was furious with him and everybody else on the coach, especially the two men who had caused the incident, since they hadn't said anything when the guide was threatening to go without Dad. For the rest of the day, whenever she saw the two men she just glared at them and refused to speak to them.

And that was our first taste of holidays abroad. However, it didn't put us off and we went to Austria – one week in the Alps for £20 – and Italy in the next couple of years, as well as continuing our tours of Britain.

CHAPTER THIRTEEN

PROFUMO, KENNEDY AND THE CUBAN MISSILE CRISIS

M y first vague awareness of politics came with listening to news stories about the Mau Mau uprisings in Kenya in the early 1950s. Of course, I didn't really understand what it was all about and some of the descriptions of 'terrorist' outrages were so graphic I sometimes worried that our prefab might be attacked by gangs of Mau Mau. This was followed by news of unrest in Cyprus and similar uprisings.

The first time I ever expressed a political opinion, I was shot down in flames by my family, but then I was only nine. This was when the Soviet Union ruthlessly put down the Hungarian uprising. The news as broadcast on radio and television had always treated those in revolt against British rule in Kenya and Cyprus as terrorists and painted a very black picture of them, so when the Hungarians rose against the Soviet Union

I assumed they were in the wrong as well, and one day, at Nan and Grandpa's, the grown-ups were tutting at the news from Hungary. When I voiced the opinion that it was all the Hungarians' fault as they had started the trouble, I was quickly told that I was too young to understand and I should keep such opinions to myself.

I can just about remember the 1959 General Election because John had obtained a free map from *The Times*, showing all the constituencies, and spent some time after the results were declared colouring it in with red for Labour, blue for Conservative and green for Liberal. But it wasn't until my early teens that I began to take a real interest in politics and what was going on in the news. Until the late 1950s, there had been few black people living in Hackney but in the early 1960s more and more West Indian families began to settle in the area as the British Government continued to encourage immigration to help staff our hospitals, public transport and so on. The numbers were still very small but more noticeable, though they meant nothing to me. It was while on the coach back from football one afternoon that I realised that the presence of black people on our streets was the subject of comment. A group of boys sitting at the back of the coach were counting the numbers of black people they saw and making what I thought were completely uncalled-for remarks about their appearance. This was the first time that I had ever encountered any form of racism and it made me feel very uncomfortable.

There was a clear polarisation of views on immigration in the school and in my class. Several boys took a strong view on immigration and were utterly opposed to it. It wasn't until the

Commonwealth Immigrants Act of 1962 that there was any control over the numbers of immigrants from Commonwealth countries. Even so, there were relatively few in and around the East End and I couldn't understand why some people were making such a big fuss about it and even more feeling the need to use such disparaging language when talking about black people. Discrimination on grounds of race was not outlawed until 1965 with the passing of the Race Relations Act, so in the early sixties it was still not uncommon for landlords to put up the sign 'No blacks, no Irish, no dogs' on the door of their boarding house. I suppose the fact I came from a Jewish background with its own history of discrimination allowed me to see this in a completely different way to those from a purely white British background, though, of course, a lot of my friends and classmates shared my views, whatever their background. There would be many informal discussions especially at break between the groups expressing opposing views.

In the third year, we had a new English teacher, Mr Dowler. Every now and then, he would suspend the normal syllabus to hold a more formal debate in class, immigration being the most frequently debated topic. At the end of the lesson, he would sum up the arguments and would invariably come down on our side.

Mr Dowler was a Canadian and not a great one for formality. Whereas most of the teachers wore their university gowns when teaching, he used to come into class wearing a beat-up old duffle coat, looking very scruffy. He didn't last more than a year and the rumour was the Headmaster had got rid of him firstly because of his unconventional dress and secondly because he was a bit of a 'lefty'.

It was during these debates that I found out which of my friends and other classmates thought like me. Fortunately, Murray and John were very much on my wavelength, as was Herbert and his friend, Colin Mitchell. Gradually, as time went on, we would talk more and more about politics in general, not just immigration and racism. By the third year, we had also got to know many of the boys in the year above us quite well and they seemed to be a real hotbed of left-wing thought. One boy in particular, Larry Burr, was a member of Hackney Young Socialists, the Labour Party's youth organisation, and he encouraged us to go along to a meeting.

So, one Friday evening, Murray, John, Herbert, Colin and I went along to Hackney Labour Party headquarters in Graham Road, just off Mare Street, to attend our first political meeting. When we got there, we found about thirty people, all crammed into a fairly small, very smoky room. Later, I was told by the Chairman that Hackney Y.S. was the largest Young Socialist group in the country if you didn't include Wigan, which was really only a social club. So we didn't count Wigan.

I have to admit that I couldn't make head nor tail of what went on for most of the meeting. We had fairly straightforward discussions at school about things within our own experience, but here there seemed to be the most complicated and esoteric discussions going on about obscure points of socialism. I was to learn a bit later on that Hackney Y.S. was the melting pot of Trotskyism. There were three main Trotskyist groupings in Great Britain at the time, which later became the Socialist Workers Party, Militant and the Workers Revolutionary Party. Some of the leading members of all three were in Hackney Y.S.

They spent more time tearing each other to shreds than they ever did berating the Tories!

Going to Hackney Y.S. became a regular Friday night activity for my friends and me. I never really did get to grips with all the intricacies of Trotskyism, but it did give me the chance to make new friends and, in spite of us not being like Wigan, there were some social activities as well – nights out at the pub and parties.

My political development coincided with the British satire boom that launched itself on a largely unsuspecting public in the early 1960s. The growing youth culture brought with it a more generalised cynicism of authority. And, although political satire had a long and honourable history in Great Britain, it was, by the time of the Second World War, largely a forgotten art, and certainly throughout the War itself, with everyone pulling together, the idea of making fun of those in charge was unthinkable.

Once the War was over, there was a general feeling of not wanting to return to the 'bad old days' of the 1930s when unemployment was rife and wages depressed, hence the landslide election of a majority Labour Government for the first time in British history. However, there was still a general deference to those in power. There were probably two things that changed all that, which, as it happened, coincided. The first was the growing independence of young people through the rock'n'roll revolution and the second was the Suez Crisis in 1956. For the first time, probably ever, the British Government embarked on a war that was not supported by the great majority of the British people. Suez resulted in a growing lack of faith in governments of all types.

The late 1950s and early 1960s saw a big cultural change in the arts as 'kitchen sink' dramas by the likes of John Osborne and Alan Sillitoe brought a new gritty realism to literature in the form of novels, plays and films, and even television got in on the act with *Coronation Street*'s first airing on 9 December 1960, followed by series such as *Z-Cars* in 1962.

While this new emphasis on portraying everyday life for working-class people was taking over from the cosy middle-class world of playwrights like Noël Coward and Terence Rattigan, another strand of the general dissatisfaction with authority began to stir in the bastion of the middle-class world itself, Oxbridge.

In particular, four young graduates from Oxford and Cambridge – Peter Cook, Jonathan Miller, Alan Bennett and Dudley Moore – shook the Establishment with their show, *Beyond the Fringe*, which premiered at the Royal Lyceum Theatre in Edinburgh on 22 August 1960 and transferred to the Fortune Theatre in London. The show broke new ground, with Peter Cook impersonating the then Prime Minister, Harold Macmillan, something unheard of at the time, and even made fun of the current craze for heroic war films. It heralded the beginning of the satire boom.

My first exposure to this came with *That Was The Week That Was*, broadcast on 24 November 1962. Quite by chance, I saw the first episode. It was broadcast late on Saturday evening and we had not long got in from the usual grandparents' run when we put the television on, and there it was. Immediately, it struck a chord with me and my newfound political interest. Of course, the programme itself caused a sensation and became the most talked-about programme on television.

Not long after that, I also discovered *Private Eye* at a time when it was mercilessly satirising the Government over the Profumo Affair. The affair concerned the sexual liaison between the Secretary of State for War, John Profumo, and a nineteen-year-old call girl, Christine Keeler, who was simultaneously involved with a Soviet naval attache, thus creating a possible security risk. Profumo made a personal statement to the House of Commons denying any impropriety but was forced to admit he had lied to Parliament a few weeks later. The repercussions of all this severely damaged the Conservative Government and to a large extent finished off the work started with the Suez Crisis in completely destroying any last vestiges of the mystique of government and the idea that middle- and upper-class politicians knew best. It encouraged ordinary young working-class people to feel that they could and should get involved more and led to my friends and me getting deeper and deeper into politics. It wasn't just something reserved for Friday nights. We now took part in local activity, canvassing, leafleting and so on, as well as national events, going on demonstrations in London behind our Hackney Young Socialists banner.

The most exciting event I took part in was when the pre-War fascist leader Oswald Mosley tried to organise a meeting in a local market street, Ridley Road, in Dalston on 31 July 1962. With the increasing number of immigrants coming into Hackney, Mosley had decided the time was right for a comeback. We were determined to stop this happening, just as our parents had done at the famous Battle of Cable Street in 1936. And so we turned out in force, along with other local Labour Parties, the Communist Party, trade union branches and so on. We easily outnumbered Mosley's supporters but they were well protected by the police.

Mosley planned to speak from the back of a lorry but, as soon as he appeared from between two police buses, we all surged forward and knocked him to the ground. The police helped him up and he climbed onto the lorry where he was met by a hail of missiles including rotten fruit, pennies and stones. His speech was drowned out by boos and a chorus of 'Down with the Fascists!' There was a continuous chant of 'BUM, BUM, BUM!' – these were the unfortunate (for him) initials of Mosley's party, the British Union Movement. Police were forced to close the meeting within three minutes and shepherd Mosley back to his car, whereupon we continued to punch and kick at the side of the vehicle as he drove off through a gangway cleared by mounted police. We were absolutely delighted with the result and the streets round Ridley Road were full of people, including us, dancing and singing Socialist songs and other chants for at least another hour.

Later that week, the local paper, the *Hackney Gazette*, published a photograph of Oswald Mosley on the ground with a demonstrator kicking him. As it happened, the demonstrator in question was one of our Hackney Y.S. members, Robin Jamieson, so the photo was cut out, framed and hung on the wall of the Labour Party office under the heading 'Robin puts the boot in'. It remained there for several years.

This sort of politics was very exciting for a fifteen-year-old and much better and more rewarding than arguing interminably about what Trotsky might have said in 1917. Not so exciting was the time the Cuban Missile Crisis came to a head.

As a result of the Second World War, two new superpowers emerged, the USA and the Soviet Union. Between them, they more or less carved up the world into their own spheres of influence and there was a standoff between the two completely differing ideologies. This was the period known as the Cold War. In order to defend themselves from possible attack by the other, both superpowers built up large arsenals of nuclear weapons. In general, the USA's sphere of influence comprised the Americas and Western Europe, while the Soviet Union had Eastern Europe and large swathes of Asia. However, in 1959, a communist revolution took place in Cuba leading to Fidel Castro being proclaimed Prime Minister and the Soviet Union gaining its first foothold in the Americas. Cuba became the source of great tension between the superpowers and an attempt was made to invade the country by Cuban exiles backed by the USA to remove Castro. This was very badly handled and completely failed in its objective.

However, it was when US spy planes secured evidence on 14 October 1962 that the Soviet Union had placed nuclear missiles on Cuba, right on its doorstep, that all hell let loose. The US President, John F. Kennedy, announced that it would not allow this and demanded they be returned to the Soviet Union. In addition, he said the USA would mount a blockade of Cuba to prevent any Soviet ships from landing in Cuba. The Soviet President, Nikita Khrushchev, replied to this by saying that a US blockade of 'navigation in international waters and air space' constituted 'an act of aggression propelling human kind into the abyss of a world nuclear-missile war'.

It was well known that several Soviet ships were en route for

Cuba and orders were sent out to US Navy ships to demand they return and to fire warning shots and then open fire on them if they did not. The whole world held its breath as this confrontation between the two superpowers continued and the prospect of the Cold War turning into a real war, and a nuclear war at that, seemed to grow ever closer.

The Missile Crisis reached its height eleven days later, on the afternoon of 25 October. It was then that the first flotilla of Soviet ships was due to meet the American blockade. On that fateful afternoon, my friends and I had Games and we were all ferried as normal to our school ground to play football. But none of us felt like playing. The atmosphere was so tense you could literally feel it; we all stood around in silence, just waiting for the news that the world was at war. We knew we would be one of the first places in line for nuclear attack as America's leading ally with nuclear weapons of our own trained on the Soviet Union, and London would be a prime target. Even the teachers didn't try to force us into playing, as they must have felt the same as we did. It was a very strange, surreal afternoon, standing around doing nothing, just waiting for the first missile to fall.

On the coach coming back, Murray said to me, 'Something must have happened as the ships should have met by now.'

This didn't cheer me up too much as, although you would have thought we'd be at war by now if the ships had actually met and the fact that we weren't could only be good news, there were all sorts of explanations that could mean it was still only a matter of time. But, as I learnt from the television news when I got home, it was good news and the Soviet Union had ordered fourteen of its ships, presumed to contain missiles, to turn round and go back home. Although this eased the tension considerably, the dispute still rumbled on for a few more days. Finally, however, on 28 October, agreement was reached to remove the missiles already in Cuba in exchange for an undertaking from the USA that it would not try to invade Cuba and overthrow Castro. The whole world breathed an almost audible sigh of relief.

One of the spin-offs from the Cold War was the space race and the continual efforts of Russia and the USA to outdo each other in this field. This was all very exciting stuff, seeing the great rockets blasting off into the heavens, and I took a great interest in what was going on as at each step the Russians seemed to get there first, with Yuri Gagarin being the first man in space, Valentina Tereshkova the first woman in space and Colonel Leonov the first man to walk in space. This led to President Kennedy's pledge that the USA would be the first country to land a man on the moon and that it would be done by the end of the decade.

Just over a year after the Cuban Missile Crisis, I returned home from Speech Day at Parmiter's and switched on the television to hear the news that President Kennedy had been assassinated. I couldn't believe it. It came as an enormous shock to the system. Kennedy had seemed to crystallise the hopes of my generation and when he was elected President it was an affirmation that the world was definitely changing and the old order giving way to the new. He was young, charismatic and a symbol of what the younger generation was capable of. We were hopeful that his election would herald a new dawn, not just in politics but the more general sense of a better world. His assassination was a shocking and bitter blow to all those hopes.

CHAPTER FOURTEEN

BEATLEMANIA, *READY STEADY GO!* AND PIRATE RADIO

Kennedy was part of the second youth revolution but, whereas the first – the mid-1950s rock'n'roll explosion – belonged exclusively to the young, which the older generation tried to avoid and denigrated at every opportunity, this second revolution caught everyone up in the sweeping changes it made to society.

Apart from the political side, it affected the whole way we lived. Everything was caught up in the changes including music, fashion, art, television, cinema – just about everything. My first realisation that a fundamental change to our way of life was underway came on 4 December 1962, just two weeks after *That Was The Week That Was* first aired. I came home from school, did my homework and put on one of my favourite television programmes of the time, *Tuesday Rendezvous*, a combination of chat, little comic sketches and music featuring early skiffle stars Wally Whyton and Bert Weedon and their puppet characters, Pussy Cat Willum, Ollie Beak and Fred Barker. As well as the regulars, most programmes featured a guest singer or singers so, when the main presenter, Muriel Young, introduced a new musical group from Liverpool, it was nothing unusual. But as soon as the song began with its wailing harmonica introduction it was clear that this was something completely new. I even shouted out to Mum, 'Come and listen to this!'

Mum looked in from the kitchen where she was preparing tea and said, 'That's different,' and stopped to listen.

The group was, of course, The Beatles.

The next morning at school, everyone was talking about The Beatles and their spellbinding performance the previous evening. It was the first time that the performance of a pop group on television had gripped everyone so completely that it was all they could talk about in the playground. It seemed obvious that The Beatles were going to carry all before them as they engulfed not just my generation but everyone.

The outward manifestation of Beatlemania were the girls who screamed at their concerts. Other pop and rock stars had had their fans of course, but there had been nothing quite like this. The Beatles changed the whole world of music and fashion. By 1963, the old rock'n'roll music scene had become quite stale and very samey, but the success of The Beatles created a whole new explosion in musical talent appearing on the scene with a completely new type of sound. They were followed by groups like Gerry and the Pacemakers, The Searchers, Billy J. Kramer and The Dakotas and Freddie and the Dreamers, who completely dominated the charts for the next couple of years. And pop music itself became big news. Before, the charts had been confined to musical papers and the young, but now they made the national newspapers and when the Dave Clark Five knocked The Beatles off the No. 1 spot one week in 1964 it was a sensation that was reported on the front page of many of the leading daily papers.

New peak-time television programmes sprang up, including *Ready Steady Go!* and *Top of the Pops*. *Ready Steady Go!* in particular became an iconic programme of its time. The show went out early on Friday evenings with the tagline 'The weekend starts here!' Even Dad gave in and let me watch it. The Mersey sound pioneered by The Beatles conquered everyone and everything.

As well as *Ready Steady Go!*, I listened to *Pick of the Pops* on the radio every Sunday afternoon. Introduced by Alan 'Fluff' Freeman with his familiar catchphrase 'Hello, pop pickers', this gave a rundown on that week's Top 20. I also bought the weekly *Record Mirror* and we would have discussions at school about which were our favourite and least favourite songs in that week's charts. Pop music was now omnipresent in a way it never had been before, and groups and the charts became a staple topic of our conversation, rivalling sport and politics.

In fact, it came home even closer to me and my friends at school as one week a record called 'Wipe Out', recorded by the American group the Surfaris, reached the Top 10. A boy in our class called Tony told us that he was in a group called The Monotones and that they were going to record a cover version of the song, which he said their producer reckoned would make the Top 10 as well. This was amazing news. A boy in our class would soon be in the Top 10, his record played on *Pick of the Pops* and quite probably we'd see him on *Ready Steady Go!* For a while, Tony basked in the admiration we all felt for him and was treated as if he was already a celebrity.

A couple of weeks later, on perusing my weekly copy of *Record Mirror*, I came across an article about a new up-and-coming group from Essex called The Monotones, together with a photograph. I looked hard at the faces in the photo but couldn't see Tony anywhere. The next day, in front of several classmates, I showed him the picture and asked him why he wasn't in it. He suddenly went pale, coughed and muttered, 'Oh… er… I wasn't feeling very well the day they took the photograph so I missed it.'

Sadly for Tony, this brought nothing but laughter and cries of, 'Oh yeah?', 'Of course, Tony!' and some other more unkind and ribald comments. Poor Tony! His celebrity world had suddenly gone pop and he never really recovered from this 'outing'.

But it wasn't just music that changed and worked its way into every facet of society and conversation. Fashions too changed and became newsworthy. Models such as Jean Shrimpton, 'The Shrimp', became superstars and celebrities in their own right. Following The Beatles' style, hair was allowed to grow longer and longer. The universal short-back-and-sides vanished forever. This obsession with new fashion was responsible for the creation of a new teenage movement, the Mods, who lived for fashion and initially looked to the clothing of top designers in France and Italy, opting for tailored suits, polo shirts and parka jackets, which became their trademark. However, when Mary

Quant introduced the mini skirt in 1964, the focus of clothing fashion changed and placed Britain right at the centre. We were moving into the era of Swinging London, when this country was at the forefront of the youth movement throughout the world and everything, music, fashion, films and television, reflected this.

Personally, I was not in tune with the new Mod fashions, being much more in sympathy with their great rivals, the Rockers, especially when the Mods adopted a very close-cut style, as I liked to wear my hair quite long. The Rockers opted for a more casual leather jacket and jeans look. I preferred this because it was much more comfortable and I couldn't really be bothered with hunting down the latest fashions. The other big difference between the Mods and the Rockers was that the Mods' chosen form of transport was the motor scooter, whereas the Rockers preferred much more powerful motorbikes, which again chimed more with my own life as an avid speedway supporter.

The two groups hated each other and large-scale fighting broke out between them. The first big set-to was at Clacton over the Easter of 1964 but very soon there were large-scale disturbances at other seaside resorts such as Margate, Brighton and Hastings. Such fracas naturally caused moral outrage in Parliament and in the newspapers too, but there is no doubt that much of the indignation was whipped up by the papers themselves with exaggerated and even downright dishonest reporting and deceptive headlines.

Although, along with everyone else, and particularly youngsters of our age, my friends and I were embroiled in the general mood of Swinging London, we never went so far as to take part in any riots at the seaside. To us, they seemed mindless and we felt that the way to change things was through our political activity and that Beatlemania and the upsurge in popular and folk music were manifestations of the young winning over the hearts and minds of the population to a better way of life that made older people more accepting of the youth of the day and showed them that young people had the energy and the will to change things. That was why the election of Kennedy in America was so crucial to this new hope and why his assassination was such a major setback.

Another phenomenon to grow out of Beatlemania was the introduction of pirate radio. The first to start broadcasting was Radio Caroline, with D.J.s such as Johnnie Walker, Emperor Rosko, 'Cardboard Shoes' Keith Skues and Tony Blackburn. Shortly afterwards, Radio London began broadcasting from just over three miles off Frinton-on-Sea, with Ed 'Stewpot' Stewart, Dave Cash, Kenny Everett and Tony Windsor. They were on for twenty-four hours a day, broadcasting non-stop pop music at a time when all you could get on BBC was *Saturday Club* for two hours on a Saturday morning and an hour of *Pick of the Pops* on a Sunday afternoon.

The start of pirate radio coincided with the beginning of the easy availability of portable transistor radios so I was able to listen to Radio London, which was my favourite station, at home in my room at night without disturbing Mum and Dad. During the holidays when Mum was at home with me, she would listen as well. Her favourite D.J. was Tony Windsor, whose show ran from 9am to 12 noon. Quite often, at about

11am, she would say to me, 'Time for elevenses and T.W.' And we'd sit down with a cup of tea – she still hadn't got round to liking coffee – and a biscuit for a half an hour or so to listen to Tony Windsor. Mum loved his trademark 'Hel-lo', with the 'Hel' being said in his normal voice and the 'lo' in a very deep voice.

For me personally, this fascination with The Beatles had another very pleasant and satisfying spin-off one night, as I was able to take advantage of this mania to ask another girl out. Her name was Maggie Steele. She was a little bit older than me and very good-looking, with dark-brown hair, hazel eyes, a lovely warm smile and a beautiful figure. In a word, she was bloody gorgeous and I fancied her like mad. She was a member of Hackney Y.S. and I had spoken to her several times but never on our own. Knowing I couldn't stand it any longer, I asked her over to the local pub after a meeting. Fortunately, she said, 'Yes, okay, I'd like that.' She didn't sound too enthusiastic but at least I had my chance now. Over a couple of pints, I chatted her up and discovered that unsurprisingly she was very keen on The Beatles. As it happened, their first film, *A Hard Day's Night*, had just been released and was showing at the Mile End Odeon, so I seized the opportunity and asked her if she'd like to come out with me to see it.

Disappointingly, she said, 'Oh, I've already arranged to see it with Anne.' (Anne was a friend of hers, who also went to the Y.S.)

We carried on talking about other things for a bit and then suddenly she said quite out of the blue, 'Of course, I could always tell Anne I'm going with you.'

I was a bit taken aback at first and it took a moment for the penny to drop that she'd gone back to my original question. Eventually, I asked, 'And will you?'

She gave me one of her warm smiles and replied, 'You know, I think I will.'

As if that wasn't enough to make my night, she then leaned across and kissed me on the forehead. I was on cloud nine. My mind was just racing. What should I say? What should I do? No words came.

Fortunately, I didn't have to say or do anything as she got up at that point and said, 'I'll have to go now but you can call for me next Friday at seven and we'll go to the pictures.'

Stupidly, I was just about to say, 'We can't go Friday, that's Y.S. night', but I just caught myself in time and instead said, 'Friday it is then.'

On the bus home from the pub, I couldn't stop thinking about her and what had just happened. The next week seemed to drag on interminably until at last Friday eventually arrived. Although it was a night my parents would be expecting me to go out anyway, I thought I would tell them what I was doing, but I was still a bit guarded about how I broke the news to them. I just said, 'I'm going to the pictures with a friend tonight to see *A Hard Day's Night* instead of the Y.S.'

Dad said, 'When you say a friend, they usually come in two sexes. Is this a male friend or a girl?'

For some reason when he put it that way, I felt faintly embarrassed and mumbled, 'Oh, it's a girl I know from the Y.S.'

Mum gave me a big smile and said, 'Well, in that case, you'd better put a nice shirt on and look smart.'

Dad said nothing. I wasn't sure whether he approved or not; Mum obviously did.

When I arrived at Maggie's house, her father opened the door and said, 'So you're Norman, are you? We've heard a lot about you.'

I wasn't quite sure what she could have said about me as we didn't really know each other that well, but it sounded very promising.

Before I could respond, Maggie came to the door and said to her dad, 'See you later.'

She lived fairly near the Odeon so we walked and as we did so she took my hand and we continued to hold hands till we got there.

There were an awful lot of teenage girls waiting to go into the cinema when we arrived and during the film itself there was such a lot of screaming going on that I didn't hear most of the film. Fortunately, Maggie didn't join in. I put my arm round her and she leaned her head on my shoulder.

After the film, we went to a nearby pub, the Bancroft Arms, for a drink (saloon bar, of course!) and then she said, 'I think we'd better get back now.' So we walked back to her house and she let herself in and said, 'Do you want to come in for a bit?' *Did I?* Put like that, this was an invitation I certainly wasn't going to refuse. She led me up the stairs to her room and asked me if I wanted a coffee. I have to say that at that particular moment coffee wasn't exactly the uppermost thought in my mind and I didn't actually answer her at all. I caught myself just staring at her.

Maggie looked at me and, as if she could read my thoughts, laughed and said, 'No, nor do I really!'

She then sat on the bed and patted the space next to her. I sat down. 'That was a really good evening,' she said, 'thank you.' She then rested her head on my chest and added, 'I'm feeling very tired,' as she dropped her head down.

As we sat there on the bed, God knows how much I wanted to kiss her, but she was looking downwards and just a bit out of reach and I was feeling quite frustrated. Suddenly, she turned her head and looked up at me, gazed into my eyes and then both together we kissed. Neither of us was first, it was a simultaneous reaction and it was just the most wonderful moment. We lay back on the bed for some time with our mouths and tongues firmly entwined.

I didn't want to spoil this moment at all but I was wondering whether I should try going a bit further and what her response would be. She was wearing quite a loose-fitting, low-cut dress and, in the position we were in, I could see quite a lot of the top of her boobs. I just really had such a strong urge to touch them but I was worried about how she would react so very slowly I moved my hand up her body to see what she would do. She did nothing to stop me but carried on kissing, so I decided I had to take the plunge and I cupped her breast with my hand. It was so soft – exactly like Terry Gregory had told us in the playground all those years ago. It was just the most beautiful feeling, being so intimate with this girl that I fancied something rotten. She still didn't do anything to stop me but I felt I didn't dare go any further as I didn't want to lose what I had, so we just stayed like this.

Sadly, not for long though, as suddenly this idyllic little cameo was rudely shattered by a loud coughing outside the door and her father's voice saying, 'Have you got that Norman in there, Maggie?'

She sat up quickly and replied, 'Oh yes, we just came back for a coffee.'

'Well, I think he'd better go now,' came the response from outside the door.

I got up quickly, gave Maggie a peck on the cheek and opened the door. 'Good night, Mr Steele,' I said as I hurried down the stairs.

Going home that evening, I was in a daze. This was my first real sexual experience and my mind was just reeling. It had been such a wonderful feeling and I couldn't help but think where this could lead to.

Sadly, the sequel to this marvellous evening was that it didn't lead anywhere. I saw Maggie a few more times but, as far as sex went, that was as good as it got. We never went back to her house again, nor did we ever come back to mine. And the opportunity didn't present itself again. A couple of months later, she went to university and I never saw her again. She didn't even write to me. I felt a bit down in the dumps that it had ended like this as I really liked her and didn't really know why she didn't want anything more to do with me but by this time there was so much else going on in my life that I didn't have a lot of time to dwell on it.

CHAPTER FIFTEEN

GOODBYE

My last year in the prefab was a traumatic year with so many events happening. I suppose it could be said to have started in March 1964 when Grandpa died. He had been taken into hospital suffering from a stomach ulcer. The following day, Dad received a phone call at work from Nan, saying that the hospital had rung to tell her that she needed to come in straight away. She sounded very agitated so he went straight off to Chingford to pick her up. Not having a telephone at home, Mum and I knew nothing of this. I had arranged to go ten pin bowling that night with the West Ham Supporters' Club so I left to get the bus to Leytonstone Bowl and had a good evening with the club.

I returned home about 10.30. Dad was already back. He took me into the big room and simply said, 'Grandpa died this afternoon.' I didn't know what to say; I had never experienced anything like this before. No one close to me had ever died before. I knew you were supposed to feel very sad at news like this but I didn't really feel anything, so I just said, 'Yeah?' Dad nodded. In a way, it didn't seem real to me and I couldn't really tell how upset Dad was. He was putting on a brave face for my sake, I think. I suppose it didn't come home to me until the following day when we visited Nan's house to make arrangements for the funeral. Keeping up the Jewish tradition really meant he should have been buried within twenty-four hours but, as he hadn't died until late in the afternoon, there hadn't been time to organise the funeral for the next day, so it was arranged for the following day.

When I arrived with Dad, Nan was almost inconsolable. She just sat in her armchair, staring into space and every now and then bursting into tears. I kept looking at Grandpa's armchair, half-expecting to suddenly see him there, but, of course, he never arrived and it was that empty chair that really brought home to me what had happened and that I would never see him again, never discuss boxing with him again, never have him call me a 'dancer's labourer' again, never have him try to knock my loose teeth out with a rolled-up copy of the *Daily Mirror*. For the first time since Dad had told me the previous evening, I felt quite sad and upset.

The funeral was held the following day. A number of relations I'd never seen before turned up, including my great-aunt Sarah, Grandpa's sister. As can be imagined, it was a very sad day, but I was struck by the beautifully clear singing voice of the cantor at the burial service. It is normal at a Jewish burial service for the eldest son to say *Kaddish*, a prayer for the departed, but, as this is spoken in Hebrew and Dad couldn't speak any of the language, Uncle Albert did it instead.

After Grandpa's body was committed, we all came back to Nan's for a cup of tea and some sandwiches. Nan and the children then all sat round in a circle as this is the next part of the Jewish custom when the closest family members sit *Shiva* for seven days. Formally, it meant they had to stay in the house and do nothing while other members of the family and community were supposed to look after them. However, because they weren't really part of any Jewish community and other members of the family had their own lives to get on with, they looked after themselves for the week, preparing their own meals and so on. I knew nothing about this seven-day mourning and hadn't realised that Dad wouldn't be coming home with us, but he stayed at Nan's for the whole week. As John, Mum and I left, we had to go round to each of the mourners, shake their hand and say, 'Long life to you.' It was a very difficult experience, especially having to say it to Nan, as she was still in tears most of the time.

Once Dad had returned from mourning, life continued much as it had done, though not for long, as later in the year we received our first indications that our time in the prefab was coming to an end. When they were first built, it was envisaged that they would just be temporary dwellings and certainly for no more than ten years. By 1964, my parents and John had been living there for eighteen years. Strangely enough, the first intimation came when we received a postcard from the Ministry of Works, which said that, if we moved, they would buy our fridge. It was a bit mystifying so the next day Mum asked our rent man when he came for his weekly rent collection if he knew anything about our moving. He replied that we would be receiving Notice to Quit early in the New Year and that we would be given six months to leave.

Although we knew that at some time we would have to move, it nevertheless came as a bit of a shock to us. Personally, I was overwhelmed by the sad news. The prefab was the only home I had ever known. It might not have been so bad for Mum, Dad and John as they had moved around plenty, especially during the War, but for me I felt devastated. All my life had been invested in that house; all my memories were there, everything I had ever known or done was tied up in the prefab. In all honesty, I felt much more heartbroken than when Grandpa had died. This time it was as though a part of me had died too. And we hadn't even been told anything official yet.

'God knows how I'm going to feel when the day we have to leave actually comes,' I thought to myself. I was not looking forward to it one bit.

It was on Monday, 8 February 1965 that we were officially told for the first time. A representative from the L.C.C. called personally to let us know we had six months to leave. As we were Council tenants, it was a matter of moving to another L.C.C. estate and he mentioned Debden, Loughton, Chigwell and Hainault, all of them in Essex, as possibilities. He said we would be hearing from him again when he had any definite houses to offer.

The first to receive an offer of a house was No. 1, who were offered a nineteenth-century council-owned house in Debden.

After going to view the property, they complained to us that the bedrooms were too small and there was no room for a wardrobe, it stood in two acres of its own ground in the middle of nowhere, obviously had a mouse infestation and was most probably haunted. They added that they had accepted the offer on the spot. On 22 March, they became the first of the original seven to leave their prefab.

By May, three more of the occupants, Polly, Bally and Copper, had moved and, three days after my eighteenth birthday, the Council pulled down Nos. 1, 2 and 3. Where there had once been three loving homes housing families we knew as friends and neighbours, who had shared our happy times living in a prefab on Millfields, all that was there now was a pile of impersonal rubble. Their loss left a big hole in our little community in more ways than one.

The sad and inevitable end was rapidly approaching and there was nothing I could do about it. As it happened, we were the last to receive an offer, when, on 2 July, a letter came, informing us there was a house available on the Debden Estate in Loughton. Dad immediately made arrangements to view it and, on 6 July, Mum and Dad returned from seeing the house to tell me that they had accepted the offer and we would be moving on 3 August. Although I had, of course, been expecting this news, having an actual date came like a hammer blow and I felt in utter despair.

As if this wasn't a big enough trauma in my life, there was still plenty to come in the month before our move. Just over a week later, a policeman came to our door one evening to tell Mum that Nanny Sinnott was dangerously ill in Guy's Hospital. As it happened, Dad was at Nanny Jacobs's house, so Mum had to get a bus to the hospital. When Dad arrived home at about half past nine, I told him what had happened and he said he would drive up to the hospital. I said, 'You'll probably pass Mum on the way back.' But he went anyway and did pass her on the way as she arrived back home at about half past ten. She told me that Nan was taken into hospital at four o'clock that morning with a cerebral haemorrhage and had been unconscious ever since.

The following day, Mum went back up to the hospital while Dad went to work and I went to school as usual. As the next day was our last day at school, I had arranged to go out with some of my friends to The Approach that evening to celebrate the end of school life, so I didn't return home till about half past ten. When I walked in the door, Dad was sitting in the armchair with his arm round Mum, who was sitting on the arm in tears.

Dad looked up at me and said, 'I suppose you can guess.'

I went over and put my arms round Mum and gave her a kiss. All she said was: 'Would you like a cup of Ovaltine?'

I said, 'It's okay, I'll do it.'

But she got up and said, 'No, *I'll* do it,' and went into the kitchen.

Dad said to me, 'Let her do it, she wants to and it'll help her.'

The next day was another big landmark as it was the day I finally left school and then, as if all that wasn't enough, on the following day, Saturday, 17 July, at the age of twenty-five, John got married to his girlfriend, Barbara. I didn't know Barbara very well as they hadn't been going out together for very long and, because of this and the fact that John didn't live at home and hadn't for many years, she had only been to the prefab on a couple of occasions. But what little I had seen of her I liked, so I was very pleased for my brother. As it happened, I nearly missed the wedding altogether. Mum and Dad had been on at me for a week or so to get my hair cut for the big day, but, what with everything else that was going on, I hadn't got round to it. On the morning of the wedding, Dad said, 'You'd better go round to Frank's and get your hair cut.'

Frank was a barber in Chatsworth Road but I hadn't used him for years. I had been involved in a fight in there with another boy called Peter West when I was about twelve – I can't remember what it was about now – but I had vowed never to go back there and went to a different barber in Chatsworth Road. When I was about fifteen and becoming more conscious of fashion and the need to look good for any girls that might come along, I switched to another hairdresser in Well Street, which was a bus ride away, but he was a much better stylist. As far as Frank and the other barber were concerned, it was just a case of short-back-and-sides and that was it – Mod fashions still hadn't quite caught up with them! No chance of a Beatles haircut or a David Frost, or anything else.

The new hairdresser in Well Street was up with all the latest fashions, so I went there now since I preferred my hair a bit longer. However, it did mean that it was going to take some time to get my hair cut as I had to get the bus to Well Street, but off I went. When I returned home, Mum and Dad had gone in the car to the wedding, leaving me a note telling me to follow on by bus. I eventually arrived, having missed the actual ceremony but in time for the buffet.

Not long after I arrived, John came over to us and asked, 'Why hasn't Nanny Sinnott come?'

Mum replied, 'She's not feeling very well today, John.' She had not and still did not tell him that she had died two days earlier because she didn't want to spoil his big day.

Mum still had one more sacrifice to make, this time for my sake. We were due to go away on holiday to Italy together on the Monday. I assumed it would be cancelled, but Mum wouldn't hear of it. Although obviously not in any sort of mood to go on holiday, she insisted we went as she didn't want to spoil things for me. As always, she had put her two children first before anything she herself might be feeling.

It did, of course, mean that she missed her own mother's funeral. On the day it took place, we were in Venice, visiting St Mark's Square. Mum was wearing a black dress. At 12 noon, the time the burial was due to take place, the bells of St Mark's Basilica tolled out the hour. It was as though they were ringing out for Nan's funeral. Mum looked up at the church and had a quiet sob for a few seconds. Then she got up, shook herself and said, 'Right, where are we going to have lunch?'

For a while, she seemed to be bearing up quite well, but a couple of days later it all got on top of her and she was really depressed and spent most of one day crying and not wanting to do anything. I think what brought it on particularly that day was that Dad and I, rather insensitively when you think about it, bought some postcards to send home and started writing them out. But I expect it was bound to come out at some time, for she had been so brave and selfless up until that point. Even then, her despondent mood only lasted for that one day, and for the rest of the trip she tried her best not to let it spoil our holiday.

After all the traumas of Nan dying, my leaving school, John's wedding and a rather fraught holiday in Italy, we returned home on Monday, 2 August for what was to be my last night in the only home I had ever known. We got up early next morning and sat down to our last breakfast in the kitchen, looking out the window onto the large plane tree and Pete's off-licence, a view that had become so familiar over the last eighteen and a bit years. Soon afterwards, the removal van arrived and all our furniture and belongings were loaded up. Now the place was empty except for Mum, Dad, Spot the cat and me.

I walked round the house, taking one last look at each room as the memories came flooding back. Eventually, Dad said, 'Shall we then?' The moment I had been dreading had finally arrived, it was really going to happen: we were going to drive away to a new home, never to set foot in the prefab again. We walked slowly down the path to the car. I got in and Dad started the engine up. As we drove off down Millfields Road, I turned and took one last lingering look at my beloved prefab till it was forever gone from my sight.

It had been an eventful year, culminating in an especially dramatic final month, but now my East End childhood was well and truly over and a new life in Loughton and at college beckoned.